My Heart will always be in the Hills

OF

NEW ENGLAND

Featuring the photography of Neil Sutherland

First English edition published by Colour Library Books Ltd.
© 1987 Illustrations and Text: Colour Library Books Ltd.
    99 Park Avenue, New York, N.Y. 10016, U.S.A.
This edition is published by Crescent Books
Distributed by Crown Publishers, Inc.
h g f e d c b a
Display and text filmsetting by ACESETTERS LTD., Richmond, Surrey, England.
Printed and bound in Barcelona. Spain by Cronión, S.A.
ISBN 0-517-405539
All rights reserved
CRESCENT 1987

NEW ENGLAND

Text by Suzi Forbes

Produced by
TED SMART and DAVID GIBBON

CRESCENT BOOKS

New England – a land of rolling hills, gentle woodlands, flowering fields, starry lakes; of villages with tree-lined streets and impressive clapboard houses with yards enclosed by picket fences; of sparkling white churches with steeples reaching for heaven; of rushing streams and mellow, lazy rivers; of white-tailed deer and beavers, raccoons, squirrels and chipmunks; of sea gulls and seals; of wildly brilliant hues of reds, oranges and yellows in the fall – a contented, civilized place – that's New England today, but it wasn't always like that!

Back in 1497, when Giovanni Caboto (known in England as John Cabot) sailed from Bristol on commission "to seeke out . . . regions . . . of the heathen," he would have found little that could be called civilized. Rugged seacoasts with rocks so large they seemed to reach out to smash his ship, and thick, impenetrable forests, totally unlike the gentle rolling countryside of England – that's what would have greeted him. And he found heathens! They were friendly, tolerant Indians from the Algonquin nation who raised corn and hunted and fished. John Cabot laid claim to the region for England and returned home to a happy King Henry VII, who rewarded him with £10 "to have a good time with."

The next explorer to reach New England was actually in the service of France. Giovanni da Verrazano, the discoverer of New York, also ventured further North. In 1524 he sailed into Narragansett Bay and continued along the coast of an island known to the Indians as Aquidneck. Impressed by the beauty of the region, he noted in his book that it reminded him of the Greek island of Rhodes. Eventually, after the town of Newport was settled, Aquidneck was renamed Rhode Island.

Long before these events took place, however, during the ice age, Verrazano's ancestors wouldn't have found even a trace of Narragansett Bay. Instead, they would have found mountains as high as the present-day Alps and Himalayas. What is left of them today is known as the Presidential Range. Mount Washington, in New Hampshire, is the highest point in New England at 6,288 ft., a far cry from the majesty it once

knew. Huge ice sheets wore it down to its present height. The enormous boulders scattered across the New England states and out into the Maine seacoast, are remnants also, as are many ponds, lakes and waterfalls. When all of the ice finally melted, it left prominent ridges of debris on the edges. These remained above sea level when the ocean invaded, and are the present islands of Martha's Vineyard, Nantucket, Block Island and Long Island.

As harsh as the glacial age had been, it left strewn among the granite ledges many patches of excellent soil – enough to support small villages and farms. The forests contained stately pines that could make knotless boards or towering ship masts. This is the land, then, that finally became home to New England's first settlers.

Back in England, things were in a religious ferment. Henry VIII had ascended to the throne in 1509 and separated the English Church from Rome. They wouldn't grant him a divorce to marry Anne Boleyn, you see. Abuses in the Catholic Church had caused general dissatisfaction anyway, and many saw this as a way to "purify" it. But ever since, things had been in a state of confusion, sometimes Roman Catholic and sometimes Anglican.

Elizabeth I came to the throne in 1558 and said ENOUGH!! She decreed that the Church of England would be the recognized church. In spite of this support and a total separation from the Pope in Rome, the Church of England remained almost identical to the Catholic Church. For those who wanted to "purify" the church, this new one just wouldn't do.

A few of the dissenters lived in the little village of Scrooby, England. They felt so strongly about it they started their own church and called themselves "Puritans." Their goal was to remain members of the Church of England, but to purify it from within. They wanted each church to be completely self-governing, by choosing its own pastor and officers. They were denounced by other groups as "democratical," the worst of all possible slanders. They really weren't democratic, though. They only admitted "Saints" to membership (those who confessed the faith and swore to a covenant). And you can be sure the ordinary rank and file were not even invited.

Other groups left England altogether. One little band found its way to Leyden, on the Dutch Coast. They believed the only way to "purify" the church, was to make a clean break with it. They were later given the name of "Pilgrim." Their years in Leyden were hard ones. They had difficulty making ends meet and they certainly didn't want their children raised Dutch! Furthermore, Holland was at war with Spain. If Spain should win the war, it could mean the Spanish Inquisition all over again.

No one seems to know how these two groups got to know each other, but when William Bradford in Scrooby negotiated a patent with the Virginia Company in 1620 to move his band to the Virginia colony, the contingent from Leyden joined them. When they set sail in the 3-masted schooner "Mayflower," the "Saints" numbered 51 of the 101 passengers. The rest were "Strangers," including "goodmen" (ordinary settlers), hired hands and indentured servants. They also took pigs, chickens and goats.

Somehow, they only lost one soul on that long, hard voyage. But, instead of landing in Virginia, as they had intended, they landed on the shore of Cape Cod. Some say it was intentional because they had heard they would not be hospitably received in Virginia. Others say they got lost. Whatever the reason, here they were on Cape Cod.

William Bradford tells us the weary emigrants "fell upon their knees and blessed ye God of heaven, who had brought them over ye vast and furious ocean." It was November, 1620 "and ye whole countrie, full of woods and thickets, represented a wild and savage heiw."

The next thing they did was really quite miraculous. The small band of male "Saints" persuaded the other men aboard ship to form themselves in "a civil body politick." The document they signed – The Mayflower Compact – became the basis of colonial law, and later of the U.S. Constitution. With it, they formed their own democratic self-government with church law as the sole code, and promised "all due Submission and Obedience" to its "just and equall lawes." Having created their own commonwealth, they then elected Deacon John Carver as the first governor chosen by free people in a free election.

Next they needed to find a permanent settlement. Cape Cod didn't seem quite right, so they scouted around and decided on Plymouth. The day after Christmas, 1620, they set foot on the land that would become the first New England town.

They knew the Lord was with them when they found this village. It had been the Indian Village of Pawtuxet only a few years earlier, but all its inhabitants, except one, Squanto, had been decimated by a "plague." Squanto became the Pilgrim's guide and advisor, showing them how to grow and use such strange crops as corn, beans and various kinds of squash, including pumpkin.

He was so successful that by the next October, the Pilgrims felt they would have a celebration. Edward Winslow, one of the "Saints," described this famous occasion to a friend in England: "Our harvest being gotten in, our Governor sent four men on fowling, that we might after a more special manner rejoice together, after we had gathered the fruit of our labors. The four in one day killed as much fowl as, with a little help beside, served the Company almost a week. At which time, among other recreations, we exercised our arms, many of the Indians coming among us, and amongst the rest their greatest king, Massasoit with some 90 men, whom for three days we . . . feasted. And they went out and killed five deer, which they brought to the plantation and bestowed on our Governor and upon the Captain and others." That first Thanksgiving has now become one of America's greatest traditions.

Although half of that small band of settlers had died during the first cold, hard winter, word reached England that the new country was not a bad place to live. More and more settlers made the crossing, and the community started to grow.

John Winthrop had been hearing a lot about the New World. He was educated at Trinity College, Cambridge, and had served as a Justice of the Peace. But things were not going well for folks in England. The thirty years war was raging. Exports were down and unemployment was up. Religious persecution was rampant. In fact, things were so bad that the period from 1630 to 1643 is known as the Great Migration. Over 20,000 people emigrated to New England and some 45,000 to the southern colonies and the West Indies. Winthrop was among them. He had a large family and with all those mouths to feed, decided in 1630 to try his luck in New England.

Winthrop and his friends established the Massachusetts Bay Colony. They were born leaders and soon had not one, but a dozen towns. They encouraged thousands to settle in New

England in the next decade. But they were an austere and uncompromising people, especially when it came to religion. The only liberty Winthrop tolerated was the liberty to do that "which is good, just and honest."

One of the first to run afoul of Winthrop was a young minister recently arrived from England in 1631. Roger Williams quickly became known as a radical and a firebrand. One of his unpopular ideas was that England had no right to give away land that rightfully belonged to the Indians. He also preached that Massachusetts shouldn't require citizens to go to church and to pay taxes to support the church. Government and religion should be separate, he said.

These views got him banished from Massachusetts altogether. So he traveled south with some of his followers until they reached a natural harbor at the head of Narragansett Bay. Here, in June 1636, he established Providence Plantation. Of course, he bought the land from the Indians first. The most remarkable precept of his new government was that his laws were civil laws only. Religious freedom was at the core. You could go to any church of your choice, or to none at all. It was up to you. It was the first time anyone had separated church from state.

Sometimes singly and sometimes in groups, others were regularly expelled from the Massachusetts Bay Colony. Notable among them was a woman named Anne Hutchinson. She is described as a woman of rare intellect, superabundant energy and great personal magnetism. While she was in England, she became a follower of John Cotton, England's leading nonconformist minister. When he fled to Massachusetts to avoid religious persecution, Anne, her husband and their 14 children followed.

Shortly after arriving in Boston, Mrs. Hutchinson set up a discussion center to analyze the sermons of Boston's ministers. She felt the ministers were neglecting the spirit of The Bible by adhering strictly to the written word, and said so. For this, she was brought to trial, found guilty of heresy and banished "as a leper."

So, in 1638 Mrs. Hutchinson and her followers moved south and founded the town of Portsmouth. Not long after that, however, she and her family seem to have moved again, to a river in current-day Westchester County, New York State, just north of New York City. History records that in 1643 she and all her household were killed by Indians. The river where she lived and the parkway that parallels it are named in her honor.

Now most of the Indians in New England were quite friendly. Nevertheless, they were becoming more and more concerned about where they fit into this new scheme of things. People were moving North into New Hampshire, West into the lush Connecticut River Valley, South to Rhode Island and North into Maine. As they went, they simply settled down wherever they pleased. That was alright for a while, but the Indians reasoned that if they allowed this to continue forever they wouldn't have any place to go themselves.

That was when the fighting began. But the Indians were no match for the settlers. In no time at all whole tribes were virtually wiped out in a series of battles. That was the end of the Indian problem, and a lot more land was available for settlement. The settlers were convinced that God had spoken again.

If God had helped them overcome the Indians, the settlers now asked Him to help them figure out how to protect themselves against future wars. The answer was divine inspiration. Leaders from Massachusetts, New Haven and Plymouth got together in Boston and signed a document they called The New England Confederation. It recognized each colony's independence, but provided for common protection. It also said that only the group as a whole could declare war or negotiate treaties. Notably absent from this confederation were Rhode Island and Maine. They were considered too liberal, you see. Who knew? One of these days the Confederation might have to battle one of them.

Life was pretty good for everyone at this point. They believed that with hard work, a piety of spirit and strict adherence to God's will, they would prosper. And they did. The only problem that anyone could see was where to find that good crop of new ministers so essential to New England life.

An early historian explained it like this: "After God had carried us safe to New England and we had builded our houses, provided places for God's worship, and settled the civil government, one of the next things we looked for and longed for was to advance learning and perpetuate it to posterity, dreading to leave an illiterate ministry to our churches when our present ministers shall lie in the dust. And as we are thinking and consulting how to effect this great work, it pleased God to stir up the heart of one Mr. Harvard to give one-half of his estate (it being in all about £1,700) towards the erecting of a college, and all his library. After him another gave 300, others after them cast in more, and the public hand of the state added the rest. The college was by common consent appointed to be at Cambridge (a place very pleasant and accommodate) and is called (according to the name of the first founder) Harvard College." That was in 1636.

The first class to graduate was in 1642 with 9 boys. There had been eleven, but two had dropped out. The courses included such heady subjects as Liberal Arts, the Learned Tongues (Greek and Hebrew) and the Three Philosophies – History, Divinity and Medicine.

Bit by bit, both enrollment and curriculum expanded. Today, almost 37,000 students attend Harvard University and its colleges. The graduate schools include such diverse courses as Dentistry, Medicine, Business Administration, Divinity, Public Health, Design, Arts and Sciences, Law and the John F. Kennedy School of Government.

With such an auspicious beginning, success seemed assured. But things didn't start out that way. To begin with, they hired Nathaniel Eaton to teach the boys. Harvard had to close altogether when he was found guilty of severely beating one of the boys in 1639.

It reopened a year later with Henry Dunster as its first president – and a substantial leader he was! Money was always a problem, so one of the first things he did was to marry the rich widow Glover – thereby assuring a continuing source of income for the fledgling college. Coincidentally, she also had a printing press, and they all knew that could be put to excellent use.

This wonderful school has always attracted a distinguished student body (including John Adams and John Quincy Adams, Theodore Roosevelt and Franklin Roosevelt and John F. Kennedy) and an equally distinguished faculty (they've included such greats as James Russell Lowell, William James and Henry Wadsworth Longfellow). It is a center of lively discussion and one devoted to research. Not only that, but the beauty of the buildings and their setting make it well worth a visit.

Harvard is really a city within a city. The lovely old buildings with ivy climbing their brick walls are surrounded by magnificent stately trees. The finest buildings are located in Harvard Yard where Massachusetts Hall dates back to 1720. It is the oldest still remaining and Harvard Hall (1766) stands opposite it. Many of the finest architects and artists in the U.S. have contributed to Harvard's ambiance and gentility. The elaborately detailed Johnston Gates and Memorial Gateway were added by Stanford White. University Hall was designed by Charles Bulfinch and Henry Hobson Richardson

contributed Sever Hall, with its ornate Romanesque facade. Most of all, don't miss the lively statue of John Harvard by Daniel Chester French that stands in Harvard Yard. Because the plaque reads: "John Harvard, founder 1638," it's known as the "statue of three lies." First, it's not of John Harvard at all, but of a student who attended Harvard in the 1880s. Second, Mr. Harvard was a benefactor, not a founder. Third, Harvard was founded in 1636, not 1638.

Education became a cornerstone of New England life, second only to religion. In 1647, Massachusetts passed a law that every town of 50 or more must have a school and a schoolmaster. All boys were encouraged to attend – not girls, however. There were a few private schools for girls, but for the most part, girls were taught reading, writing and arithmetic by their mothers at home.

Young girls really didn't need to know much about business matters anyway, they reasoned, and they certainly weren't going to be ministers. What mattered was knowing how to sew, cook, care for children and tend the house. The charming samplers created by young girls of 9 and 10 attest to their dexterity with a needle, as they learned all the embroidery stitches they would later use on children's dresses, pillowcases, tablecloths and napkins. Not only that, they learned an important moral message at the same time. The samplers are full of verses such as:

> "Virtue and wit with Prudence join'd
> Define the manners, form the Mind
> And when with Industry they meet
> The Female Character is complete."

> "Next unto God dear Parents I address
> Myself to you in humble thankfulness
> For all your care and charge on me bestow
> The means of learning unto me allow'd
> So on I pray and let me well pursue
> These golden arts the vulgar never knew."

Life in New England centered around the home and family and village life created a close bond among neighbors. In case of illness, for example, the family doctor would pay a house call, sometimes riding as many as 10-15 miles on horseback. Often as not he would find a neighbor already there, making the sick one comfortable, cooking or helping with the rest of the family.

Barn raisings were familiar sights in colonial New England. A barn for livestock, hay and tools was essential to a New England farmer. With fire prevention practically nonexistent, however, barns were frequently going up in flames. All hands gathered when that happened to an unfortunate neighbor! With good old Yankee spirit, the men would arrive with hammer, nails, saws and lots of brawn. The women came too. They brought home baked breads, baked beans, Indian pudding, stewed pumpkin, roast duck with cranberry sauce, or maybe chicken or roast beef (or all three), succotash and steamed clams. While the men worked, the women would prepare a midday meal that makes the mouth water just to think about it. Often all this tasty food would be washed down by mugs of cider, served from pewter pitchers.

The clams they brought would have been steamed in the old Indian way by building a fire on a layer of stones near the beach. By the time they had dug lots of clams, the wood would have burned away and left hot stones, like coals. The next step was to cover the stones with seaweed, lay the clams on this and add another layer of seaweed for good measure. The clams steamed in this natural salt water had a flavor unmatched.

After the feast was over, the men would return to their work and the women, likely as not, would sit down in the comfortable living room to work on their sewing or to perhaps have a quilting bee. Fabric was scarce in New England, so bits and pieces were saved, often going into quilts. These scraps were cut into geometric shapes and sewn together. When one woman had patched together the colorful top piece, she'd call all her friends and they'd have a party. The quilting of the top layer to the bottom, with filling in between, was often the most laborious part. The women would sit in a large square and each work on the side of the quilt nearest her. The finished quilt might then be presented to a young girl as a wedding present, or to a young man on his 21st birthday. Conversation at these events was always lively, and as they quilted the pieces together, one can imagine them discussing local gossip, family history or even the latest political situation. The quilts that have survived are wonderful testimony to a hard-working, thrifty group.

New England villages followed a general pattern in their design. All the necessary elements of village life were laid out around the village green or "common." The church, usually of white clapboard with a tall steeple and belltower, would be prominently located at one end. A fine house for the preacher and his family was located next door. Elsewhere around the common, one would find a general store, a meeting house, the schoolhouse and homes of the village gentry. The village green was the pride of the community. There might be a bandstand for entertainment on Sunday afternoons. The town militia practiced their drills on the

common with the children either watching on the sidelines or following along behind. It was a pastureland for cattle and sheep. Picnics were held here in summer weather. Young lovers carved their initials in the large spreading oak trees and, on Sunday afternoons, families met to exchange pleasantries on their way home from church.

The general store was filled with all kinds of wonderments to delight the eye and nose. Fresh produce from the farm, apples and potatoes in big barrels, beef jerkey, flour, sugar, spices, salt, hard candy, jams and jellys could all be found. There was tobacco in cans, as well as tea. Bolts of printed calico would be stacked high and could be matched with buttons, thread and ribbons for a new dress. Even boots and shoes, gloves and hats could be purchased from the store. Hundred-pound sacks of flour came in pretty printed fabrics that the thrifty housewife would later use for a child's dress or dishtowels. Nothing was wasted. And if three little girls showed up in church one day with the same dress on, no one minded at all.

By the late 17th century, the first simple one-room wooden frame houses had evolved into a two story building. The newer houses would have been clapboard also, generally with a massive central chimney. Inside one would find exposed beams, rough plaster walls and a steep stairway next to the chimney. A one-story lean-to at the rear, was often referred to as the "saltbox," because its steep roof line resembled the outline of a box of salt.

Furniture in colonial times would have been rough and heavy, and generally constructed of oak. Tables, chairs, bible boxes and chests were ornamented with painted flowers or geometric motifs.

Colonial cooking was an experiment in inventiveness. The iron pot was the most important utensil. It had a hook by which it hung over a pole in the fireplace. This pole was made of green wood to prevent it from burning easily. Nevertheless it had to be checked frequently, or the unsuspecting housewife might find her dinner dumped unceremoniously into the fire.

Thank goodness this didn't last forever! After iron became more plentiful, someone figured out a way to attach the pot to a crane. The crane had ratchets that allowed the housewife to raise or lower it and to swing it out into the room so she could look inside without singeing her eyelashes. Now that was progress!!

Many typical New England towns still remain today, sometimes as though time stood still. If you visit Lexington,

Mass., for example, you can close your eyes and, if your imagination is vivid enough, open them again in the 17th century.

Although every village had its own schoolhouse and young boys were getting a reasonably good education, Harvard was really the only college in town, Cambridge or any other, for some time. But, finally, wise men reasoned that a little competition would be healthy, and more boys could be educated as well, if another college was started. So, in 1701 a charter was issued to establish the Collegiate School in Saybrook, Connecticut. Many thought that Harvard just wasn't "spiritual" enough. They were teaching subjects that weren't absolutely necessary for a preacher to know. This new college would concentrate on more conservative subjects and would avoid the distractions of Boston. The eminent puritan clergyman, Cotton Mather, was elected first president of the new college.

He explained the misfortune of Harvard thusly: "The greatest disadvantage under which Harvard labours is the proximity of Boston. The allurements of this metropolis have often become too powerfully seductive to be resisted by the gay, and sometimes even by the grave, youths who assemble there for their education. Since the erection of the West Boston bridge, the distance between the towns of Boston and Cambridge is reduced from five to little more than three miles. This fact, as I have been informed by the Governors of the University, has rendered the evil alluded to still greater. The bustle and splendor of a large commercial town are necessarily hostile to study. Theatres, particularly, can scarcely fail of fascinating the mind at so early a period of life."

Cotton Mather's school would avoid these fascinations altogether. Saybrook was a lovely little town at the mouth of the Connecticut River. There were certainly no diversions there. But perhaps Reverend Mather felt this was still too close to the evils of Boston, for in 1716 the school was moved to the New Haven green and renamed Yale in honor of the writer and diamond merchant Elihu Yale, who had donated books, three bales of goods, a picture of King George I and other sundries to get the college started. They said of Mr. Yale: "Born in America, in Europe bred/ In Africa travell'd and in Asia wed,/ Where long he liv'd and thriv'd, in London died."

Perhaps also, Cotton Mather moved the college because he felt Saybrook was still too close to Salem, Massachusetts, where he had recently stirred up such a commotion. The Puritan fusion of church and state required that ministers interpret the Bible as law. Judges then applied these opinions as commonwealth law. Failure to follow this "gospel" law often meant brutal punishment. But opposition mounted in spite of floggings and hangings of Quakers and Baptists. Besides that, many were agreeing with Roger Smith of Rhode Island that church and state should be separate. Well!! That was a direct challenge to the authority of the very powerful ministers.

To bring the focus of everyone back to the church where it belonged, and to "purify" Christian thought again, Cotton Mather, himself a student of sorcery, wrote a series of papers that revived the people's fear of witchcraft. The result was disastrous.

In 1692 several young girls of Salem whose imaginations were stirred by tales of voodoo told them by a West Indian slave, began to have visions and convulsive fits. The doctor was called. He claimed they were the victims of witchcraft. That started the panic that caused over 200 persons to be accused of witchcraft, 150 were imprisoned and 19 found guilty and hanged. It was a general hysteria that was later replaced by public grief and repentance. Twelve jurors confessed they made an "error," but it was too late for the 19 condemned.

Political problems were beginning to occupy people's minds now too. England was becoming more and more convinced that she was losing control over the New Country. Her response was to elicit ever tighter controls. Furthermore, she needed money. The answer was taxes.

In 1765 the Stamp Act was passed. Previous forms of taxation had been for the purpose of discouraging foreign imports, such as sugar and molasses. England reasoned that if the tax on sugar from France was too high, the colonies would buy English sugar instead. This new stamp tax, however, was a tax on goods made within the colonies. It applied even to newspapers, pamphlets, legal documents, playing cards, licenses and almost anything that touched on everyday life.

Well, the colonists didn't like that one bit! Especially since they had no control over it. It was the English Parliament, who didn't know anything about the New World, who were imposing this tax. Massachusetts and Connecticut didn't even have the right to send someone to England to argue against it.

The discontent mounted. Mobs burned records in the vice admiralty court, looted the home of the Comptroller of Customs and burned the Governor's mansion. John Adams stated the situation succinctly: "Our pulpits have thundered, our Legislatures have resolved, our Towns have voted, the

Crown Officers have everywhere trembled." Even the commander of the British forces, General Thomas Gage wrote home that the colonists had swallowed an overdose of the "Spirit of Democracy."

The Stamp Act was finally repealed, but only to be closely followed by the even more odious Townshend Act. This time the tax was on the import of glass, paper, tea, lead and paints. The money raised would be used for "Defraying the charge of the administration of justice, and government, in such provinces where it shall be found necessary." What was left over could be used to offset the expense of maintaining troops in America.

Once again a great commotion was raised. In Massachusetts, Samuel Adams and James Otis got the Massachusetts House of Representatives to denounce the Acts as a case of "taxation without representation." Young John Adams was in the audience and described the scene: "My eyes were constantly on the drama before me. Mr. Otis was transformed by speaking. One forgot he was plump, round-faced, short-necked; one saw only that he had the eye of an eagle, a voice and style worthy of antiquity. I can imagine Cicero spoke like him! His view of the attitude of England toward the colonies seemed to me, as he unfolded it, incontrovertibly true. And a contest appeared to me to be opened to which I could foresee no end, and which would render my life a burden, and everything – property, industry, everything! – insecure!" In 1770 all the Townshend Acts were repealed except the one on tea.

Since most New Englanders came from good English stock, they had been raised on tea. Coffee tasted bitter by comparison. But a good cup of tea in the afternoon just made the day right. This tax on tea was a source of mounting resentment.

England's response to the growing unrest was to send troops to Boston to enforce the law. The troops had nowhere to stay but with the townsfolk. And this really made the people mad. Not only did they have no say in their taxation, but now they had to house British soldiers in their homes as well!

Hostility kept mounting and finally exploded. On March 5, 1770 a number of Boston citizens met in front of the State House to protest recent events. The Redcoats were always on hand to keep things under control, but one officer lost his composure and responded to an insult with the butt of his musket. The crowd stormed the officers and the guard had to be called out. And that certainly wasn't the end of it! Several Redcoats loaded their muskets and fired into the crowd,

killing five men. "From that moment," Daniel Webster later asserted of the Boston Massacre, "we may date the severance of the British Empire."

Things calmed down for a while. In fact, they were sometimes downright cordial. But an undercurrent – a desire for independence – was always present. Finally, three years after the Boston Massacre, another incident took place. And that one inflamed the citizens to total rebellion.

The tax still remained on New England's precious tea. And because of the tax, the British East India Company had a monopoly to sell tea in the colonies. The Puritans hated the tax and the price of the tea. The anger and resentment of the average citizen knew no limits. In November, 1773, three ships from the East India Company arrived in the Boston harbor, loaded with tea.

Notices and signs sprang up on tree trunks and walls:

"Friends! Brethren! Countrymen! That worst of plagues, the detested tea is now arrived in this harbor.

Every friend to his country is now called upon to meet at Faneuil Hall at nine o'clock this day at which time the bells will ring, to make an united and successful resistance to this last, worst and most destructive measure of administration."

As much as Bostonians loved their tea, they refused to allow the captains to unload the cargo. Eventually, after a month of negotiations, the English and the Bostonians met in Old South Meeting House on December 16, 1773 to try to resolve the issue, but the meeting broke up with no satisfactory solution in sight. Sam Adams felt that a compromise simply could not be reached. It was time to take the matter in hand – and they did. Ninety men disguised as Indians boarded the ships and dumped the 15,000 pounds of tea into the bay.

Well, you can imagine how the English felt about that! The Boston merchants certainly weren't going to pay for tea that rested on the bottom of the harbor. And England did want to be paid. In retaliation, England closed the port of Boston to all shipping. Rather than bringing the people of Boston to their knees, however, this action simply hardened their resolve. The battle lines were drawn now. There would be no turning back.

As for Boston's immediate plight, good old Yankee spirit prevailed. If the British closed the port of Boston, then Boston would simply get supplies and food by land. All the other colonies united to send help to their brave Boston compatriots. Unfortunately, it was never quite enough.

As Boston suffered, the rest of the country sympathized. Finally, September 5, 1774, the thirteen colonies called a meeting to decide what to do. They called it a "Continental Congress." John Adams called it a "nursery of American Statesmen." What the 56 delegates decided was that as free subjects of the King they should have a right to determine their own future. Also, the right to govern and tax themselves, and to *not* have those soldiers in their homes if they didn't want them.

Old England didn't like this one bit! The order was issued to arrest John Hancock and Samuel Adams and send them back to England for trial. No American trial for them, where they would probably get a sympathetic jury. They'd show those troublemakers!

In April 1775, word reached the Americans that General Gage planned an attack against the village of Concord. He knew that was where John Hancock and Samuel Adams were, and he had heard that a cache of weapons was stored there. The trouble was that no one knew whether the British would leave Boston by land or come across the water. A sexton hung a lantern in the belfry of Old North Church in Boston, signaling the route and Paul Revere rode on horseback across the countryside warning the people that the British were coming.

Paul Revere saved the day. All along the 32 mile route he stopped at farmhouses and villages crying out alarm. He warned Adams and Hancock in plenty of time. The local militias drew up their battle lines. There were merely a handful of farmers and merchants against 700 British.

In Lexington, right next door to Concord, they had been expecting something like this. Seventy-seven minutemen had spent the night at the Buckman Tavern and were rallied early by their leader, Captain Parker. He advised them: "Stand your ground, don't fire unless fired upon, but if they mean to have a war, let it begin here!" And it did. Shots rang out. Americans and British lay dead. The "shot heard 'round the world" was the start of the American Revolution.

Paul Revere recorded what happened: "…We passed through the militia. There were about fifty. When we had got about one hundred yards from the meeting-house, the British troops appeared on both sides of it. In their front was an officer on horseback. They made a short halt; when I saw and heard a gun fired, which appeared to be a pistol. Then I could distinguish two guns, and then a continual roar of musketry." Paul Revere was captured.

Meanwhile, in Concord, the militia had lined up near the Old North Bridge. The Redcoats advanced from Lexington to Concord, and once again, shots rang out. But by this time, the British were exhausted and soon retreated back toward Boston, plagued by fierce sniper attacks all the way. Even a fresh contingent of 1000 new troops couldn't halt the retreat. And thus ended the first day of the Revolution. The British had suffered 273 casualties and the rebels 93.

Perhaps nowhere has that first day of the American Revolution, including Paul Revere's Ride and the spirit behind it, been better described than in Henry Wadsworth Longfellow's poem, "Paul Revere's Ride." It ends:

> "You know the rest; in the books you have read,
> How the British regulars fired and fled,
> How the farmers gave them ball for ball,
> From behind each fence and farmyard wall,
> Chasing the redcoats down the lane,
> Then crossing the fields to emerge again
> Under the trees at the turn of the road,
> And only pausing to fire and load …
> So through the night went his cry of alarm
> To every Middlesex village and farm,
> A cry of defiance, and not of fear,
> A voice in the darkness, a knock at the door,
> And a word that shall echo for evermore!
> For, borne on the night-wind of the Past,
> Through all our history, to the last,
> In the hour of darkness, and peril, and need,
> The people will waken and listen to hear
> The hurrying hoof-beats of that steed,
> And the midnight message of Paul Revere."

The battles in Lexington and Concord changed the contest from a local, political one to a national war. Virginia patriots, Pennsylvania minutemen, men from New York, Rhode Island and Connecticut all rallied to the cause.

Rebel military leaders were a mixed lot to say the least. There was Henry Knox, the Boston bookseller who learned about artillery from books, and Israel Putnam, a nearly illiterate farmer, with more daring-do than sense, and the dapper Boston physician, Joseph Warren, who died in battle in his "fine silk fringed waistcoat."

The British now held Boston itself, but they were surrounded by Americans. In a surprise move on June 16, 1775, however, some 1600 Americans sneaked in at night and occupied Breed's Hill, directly across the bay from downtown Boston. The British couldn't allow that to last for long! Under the command of General Howe, the Redcoats attacked. They got into formation, and like the gentlemen they were, simply marched up the hill to retake it. The American commander knew his troops had little ammunition and cautioned: "Don't fire until you see the whites of their eyes!" That resulted in a heavy barrage at close range and a lot of Redcoats who would never fire a musket again.

Once more General Howe commanded his men to form their precise lines, and to the familiar English drum cadence, marched them up the hill. The same thing happened a second time. On the third try, though, the British did finally take Breed's Hill through hand to hand combat. The patriots were out of gunpowder and were reduced to using stones and sticks. The British paid a very dear price for recapturing Breed's Hill. More than 10 percent of their officers killed during the entire war died on Breed's Hill that day.

Meanwhile, a second Continental Congress, held in Philadelphia on May 10, 1775, had designated these rebel troops a "Continental Army" and had selected a commander-in-chief to lead them. He was Colonel George Washington from Virginia, who was immediately promoted to General. He promptly left for Boston. On arrival, it was apparent to him that he had more to do than he had thought. He had a total of 3,500 troops. When he saw them he angrily wrote: "Such a dirty, mercenary spirit pervades the whole that I should not be at all surprised at any disaster that may happen."

Troops weren't Washington's only problem. He needed guns. But he knew where to find them! The British had lots of artillery at Fort Ticonderoga on Lake Champlain. A former druggist and supreme egotist, Benedict Arnold, was selected to capture the Fort. But Ethan Allen and his Green Mountain Boys of Vermont beat him there. The two commanders eyed each other warily. Both were sure that they should be in command, but finally agreed to issue joint orders to attack. They took the Fort and the guns. Oddly enough, of these two military leaders, Ethan Allen would later offer the British a separate peace treaty if they would recognize Vermont as a sovereign country, and Benedict Arnold would later betray his country by selling military secrets to the British.

The real hero of Fort Ticonderoga was the unassuming bookseller, Henry Knox. He somehow loaded 60 cannon and mortars on ox-drawn sledges and brought them across rivers and through forests in the middle of winter to General Washington just outside Boston. On the night of March 4,

1776, Washington had them mounted on Dorchester Heights, pointed directly at the British command. That was too much for General Howe. He really didn't want his troops annihilated. So he decided to pull out of Boston with nary a fight, and off he went! Not much of the war was fought in New England from that time on.

Some of America's greatest rebels and patriots were native New Englanders who spent the majority of the revolution elsewhere. One, in particular, had been born in Boston in 1706 but had run away to New York as early as 1723. His name was Benjamin Franklin.

Benjamin was born to Josiah and Abiah Franklin on January 6th – the 8th of 10 children of this union and the 15th of 17, if you count his step-brothers and sisters. The elder Franklin made soap and candles.

Although he had only two years of formal schooling, Benjamin read everything in sight and wrote prodigiously. At 12 he wrote "The Light House Tragedy," a short news story, and hawked it on the street to earn a little extra money.

It was at this same time that he was apprenticed to his 21 year-old brother, James, who was a printer. In exchange for £10 James agreed to teach the youngster everything he knew about the printing business as long as Benjamin stayed until he was 21. Benjamin learned quickly and soon was acknowledged as the best printer in Boston.

But Benjamin wasn't happy with this situation. He wanted some money and recognition of his own. Under his contract he couldn't be paid for his work on the newspaper until he was 20 years old. So, at 17, he decided to run away.

History records that Franklin was a ladies' man, but his escape from Boston had a touch of rascality to it. He explains: "My friend Collins, therefore, undertook to manage a little for me. He agreed with the captain of a New York sloop for my passage, under the notion of my being a young acquaintance of his that had got a naughty girl with child whose friends would compel me to marry her and therefore I could not appear or come away publicly. So I sold some of my books to raise a little money, was taken on board privately, and, as we had a fair wind, in three days I found myself in New York."

Now, New York at this time was much smaller than Boston. While Boston had two newspapers, New York had none. In fact, there was only one printer. He had no work for Franklin so he sent him on down to Philadelphia to his son's printing plant. There Benjamin found work, friends and prosperity.

Franklin's greatest talent was his ability to persuade people to work hard and to work together to make dreams come true. He worked to repeal the stamp act and for the Declaration of Independence. On a local scale, he helped Philadelphia establish the first library, the first public hospital, the first fire insurance company and the University of Pennsylvania.

As a researcher and inventor, Franklin invented the Franklin stove, bifocal glasses, a two faced clock and conducted extensive research into electricity. He also introduced rhubarb to America, studied the effect of the environment on pigeons and researched silkworms as a potential colonial crop.

As a statesman, Franklin spent the better part of 30 years in London and Paris. He was, at various times, agent for Pennsylvania, Massachusetts, New Jersey and Georgia and was largely responsible for France's decision to send men, money and guns to America during the revolution.

Another native Bostonian left home for quite another reason. John Adams was born of a rather undistinguished family of rural farmers. His parents, John and Susanna, like their parents before them, had orchards of fruit trees, fields of corn and hay, and chickens for eggs, pigs for bacon, cows to milk and, of course, horses for transportation. When John was born in 1735, his parents were determined that he should go to Harvard and become a clergyman. As it turned out, John did go to Harvard, but he became a lawyer, not a clergyman.

John met Abigail Smith, the daughter of Reverend William Smith, when she was 17. John was 27 and a rather bookish attorney. He sometimes practiced in Boston, but most often traveled the "circuit" from Weymouth to Braintree, and Hingham to Duxbury and back again. Their courtship lasted some 2 years, and was characterized by long absences from one another – a pattern that was to continue throughout their marriage.

These absences made letter-writing a necessity. Abigail was a precocious girl – intelligent, quick-tongued and direct. She had received a good education from her father and had charm, wit and a "saucy" character. John and Abigail's letters to one another are a fascinating chronicle of the important roles they were to play in shaping America, and of their love for one another.

Events in Boston, the hotbed of British opposition, formed young John Adams life. He felt the tug of independence and,

with his cousin, Samuel Adams, became one of the leading "Sons of Liberty."

When the first Continental Congress was called, John Adams was asked to take part. He wrote to Abigail: "Ay, Nabby ... A messenger rode hard from Salem to our meeting . . . There's a new and grand scene opening before me! A Congress! Ay, a Continental Congress is to meet on the first day of September at Philadelphia. So well have our Committees of Correspondence functioned, so quick has the work been got from one to 'tother. Cushing, Bob Paine, Cousin Sam Adams and myself are appointed Delegates from this province ... Ah, this will be an assembly of the wisest men upon the continent. I feel myself unequal to this business!"

It was this humility, and yet a zeal for the task that made the Adams family remarkable. John Adams never forgot his humble beginnings, and no matter how elevated his position, he never lost his longing for a simple, country life. At one point he wrote to Abigail, "My refreshment is a flight to Braintree, to my Cornfields and Grass Plotts, my Gardens and Meadows – my Fancy runs about you perpetually, frequently takes a walk with you and your little prattlings. We walk all together up Penns Hill, over the Bridge to the Plain, down to the Garden . . ."

Adams often worried that his service to his country would be detrimental to his family. Had Abigail not shared his feelings, and had John not considered Abigail an equal, history might have been recorded differently. In one of Abigail's favorite letters John said: "My dear Partner, I must entreat you to take a part with me in the struggle ... I have a Zeal at my heart for my Country and her friends which I cannot smother or conceal. This Zeal will (may) prove fatal to the Fortune and Felicity of my Family." Indeed, although John and Abigail's oldest son, John Quincy, would follow in his father's footsteps, two other sons were to become alcoholics.

John Adams, this son of Boston, was later to go on to become the first Vice President of the United States, serving under President Washington, and the second President. He helped write the Declaration of Independence and the U.S. Constitution. He served in diplomatic posts in France and England. His son, John Quincy, was to become the sixth President of the United States. By an incredible coincidence, John Adams and Thomas Jefferson, the third U.S. President, died the same day – July 4, 1826 – exactly 50 years after the signing of the Declaration of Independence.

The Boston of John and Abigail's day was a city of learning and gentility. It was larger than either New York or

Philadelphia. And of all the cities in the United States then or now, its shape has probably been changed by man most dramatically.

When founded in 1630 by John Winthrop, Boston consisted of a peninsula called Shawmut. It was connected to the mainland by a narrow, sandy neck of land. Living conditions on the peninsula kept getting more and more crowded. Gradually, the area around the peninsula was filled in. Beacon Hill, for example, was once a steep mountain with a searchlight on top. It was reduced in size to make it suitable for residential use. The leftover dirt was used to fill in North Cove.

In 1833, still more land was filled in to form South Cove. Eventually, in 1819, Back Bay was filled in as well, enclosing a total of 580 acres. This area became a fashionable residential area of broad, straight avenues lined with magnificent Elm trees. Fine Victorian mansions line the streets, many with their original stoops and elaborate wrought iron railings. The Esplanade along the Charles River is a wonderfully pleasant place to stroll on a sunny afternoon. Or you might prefer to sit on one of the many benches in the grassy park along Commonwealth Avenue. Newbury Street, with its fashionable shops and restaurants, leads to the latest redevelopment in Boston, Prudential Center and Copley Square. Here one finds department stores, elegant hotels, restaurants, plazas and office towers. Lewis Mumford calls Back Bay "the outstanding achievement in American urban planning for the 19th Century."

Some of Boston's greatest architecture happily greets the world from Copley Square. Trinity Church, started about 1877, is the masterpiece of architect Henry Hobson Richardson. It's a wonderful melange of turrets and columns and bricks and stones and towers. The inside is considered to be one of the greatest achievements of artist John LaFarge, who lavishly painted the walls and ceilings. The entire interior has a warm, rosy hue.

Opposite Trinity Church is the Boston Public Library, designed by McKim, Mead and White in 1895. With its elaborate wrought iron lanterns, bronze statues and detailed gates, it is a Renaissance Revival masterpiece. Inside, its tall arched windows bathe the main reading room with light and its high vaulted ceilings and antique red-shaded lamps, make it the perfect place to spend a cozy afternoon.

If you walk down Commonwealth Avenue to Arlington Street, you'll find yourself at the edge of the Public Garden. Walk inside to see neat lawns, flower gardens and trim paths

leading to a man-made lake. One of the delights of Boston, the Swan Boats, can be found carrying passengers on the lake's placid water.

Next to the Public Garden is the oldest public park in the United States. It's called The Common and it's the heart of Boston. As in smaller New England villages the common was originally used as a pasture and parade ground. In the 17th century a stocks, pillory and gallows were erected to discourage "malefactors." It's odd to note that the first person to use the stocks was the carpenter who built them. The town fathers thought he had charged too much! About that same time, the common was the only place in Boston where smoking was allowed. Today, it's a delightful green used by picnickers, runners, frisbee players, dog walkers and smokers.

The Freedom Trail meanders past many of Boston's historic landmarks and starts at The Common. Stroll from here along the red line that marks it, past the Old Granary Burying Ground, where James Otis, Samuel Adams, Paul Revere, Thomas Paine and Mother Goose are buried. You might even get a permit to make a rubbing from one of the old headstones.

On the corner of Washington and School Streets, you'll find the Old Corner Bookstore. For years in the 19th century, this was the meeting place of Boston's most notable writers. Longfellow, Emerson and Hawthorne all knew it well. It is now a museum and offices for the Boston Globe. As part of their excellent restoration, you can view historical diaries and newspapers.

Just across the street is Old South Meeting House, where Samuel Adam's and John Hancock's fiery oratory led to the Boston Tea Party. Most of the interior of this plain, brick building is original. Only the pews are not. The originals were used as firewood by the British during their occupation, when they used it as a riding school.

At the end of Devonshire Street, the Old State House stands adorned with the symbols of the English Crown, the lion and the unicorn, mute testimony to the fact that this was, at one time, the seat of English government in the New World. It's a stately brick building dating back to 1713. It was in front of the Old State House that the Boston Massacre took place.

Faneuil Hall (pronounced Fan-l by those in the know) over on State Street, was built in 1742. It was a marketplace and town meeting hall throughout the Revolutionary War. The cupola on top is the location of that famous symbol of the Port of

Boston, the grasshopper. It's a gilded bronze weathervane, modeled after one atop the Royal Exchange in London.

After Faneuil Hall, don't miss the series of shops, restaurants, food stands and flower stalls that make up Faneuil Hall Marketplace, with the Greek Revival Quincy Market as its centerpiece. Everything from old prints of Historic Boston and sheet music from the 1930s to donuts, sandwiches, fresh fruit and beer can be purchased. Benches set in cobblestone courtyards among trees and planters of flowers, are a welcome place to relax. Street musicians entertain. You can even buy tickets to the theater or the Boston Pops. From the Market, it's an easy walk to the waterfront where warehouses have been converted to apartments, new hotels are springing up and Boston is appreciating a new interest in its waterfront.

This might be a good place to stop and have one of the most traditional of all Boston dishes, Boston baked beans. It's a wonderful, aromatic combination of beans, brown sugar, molasses, onion and salt pork. You can get a good bowl or cup in one of the waterfront pub restaurants, or, if you are lucky enough to be invited to someone's home, you might find that it was prepared in the following manner.

A good Boston housewife will tell you that almost any kind of beans can be used. Some prefer Great Northern beans or yellow-eyed beans or white pea beans. Every housewife has her own recipe too, but none are simple. A typical one might include 1 pound of dried beans dropped into 1 quart of boiling water. They should boil for about 2 minutes and then soak in the water overnight. Next add 1 onion and a teaspoon of salt and bring to a boil again. This time simmer for 1 hour, or until the beans are tender. Drain and reserve the liquid. Mix ½ cup dark molasses, ¼ cup brown sugar, 1 tablespoon dry mustard, a bit more salt and freshly ground black pepper. Stir 2 cups of the bean liquid into the molasses and mix all together with the beans. Put an onion in the bottom of a heavy crockery bean pot and pour in the beans. Score the fatty side of ½ pound salt pork and push it into the bean mixture. Cover the beans and bake them in a 250° oven for 5 hours. Uncover and bake 1 more hour. The results will be well worth the time and trouble. It's a fragrant, delicious and hearty family meal.

Meanwhile, back on the Freedom Trail, one more stop shouldn't be missed. The Old North Church, built in 1723, is fashioned after those by Christopher Wren, so beloved by the English in London. It is a lovely, graceful church, with a slender steeple, reaching for heaven. The steeple that Paul Revere made famous has had an odd history, though. It was added when the church was 15 years old. Building steeples in

those days was tough work. Since they didn't have cranes, or even exceptionally long ladders, they built the steeple from within. As the steeple grew ever higher, the space got more and more confining. Finally, the weathervane was pushed up through the hole and fastened tightly. In the case of the Old North Church, a hurricane blew it down in 1804, and a new one, 15 feet shorter, was added by the renowned architect, Charles Bulfinch. That one blew down in 1954 too, but this time at least they used a crane to put up the new one.

A tour of Boston couldn't be complete without a walk around Beacon Hill. Its narrow, cobblestone streets, with even narrower brick sidewalks, are still lighted by gas lamps. The mellow brick Federal-style townhouses, with their lacy wrought iron balconies and weathered wooden shutters look much as they did in the 1900s. Trees line the street, graceful bay windows reach out for more light, and inside, classic Adam fireplaces can be glimpsed by the alert passerby. Louisburg Square is a refined example of the finest Beacon Hill has to offer. It's a small private park, circled by a wrought iron fence and surrounded by elegant Greek Revival townhouses.

In Boston, if you can trace your ancestry back to the Mayflower, as many can, you're a genuine "Proper Bostonian." They live the proper Boston life on Beacon Hill or in Back Bay. John Collins Bossidy said in 1910:

> "And this is good old Boston,
> The home of the bean and the cod,
> Where the Lowells talk to the Cabots,
> And the Cabots talk only to God."

But one thing about Boston is certain, not all Bostonians are "proper." And not all can trace their ancestry back to the Mayflower. The Irish are a good example. Ireland was in the midst of the greatest potato famine of its history in 1848. Ireland was a poor country anyway. Without potatoes – the staple in their diet – the people simply couldn't survive. Over a million people died in a span of five years. Rather than starve, many of the young and able men emigrated to other countries. One and one-half million in all! Tales of jobs and opportunities and wealth in New England enticed many of them. They came to Boston in droves.

For example, in 1847, Boston had a population of 260,000, including 5,000 Irish. Ten years later the population had reached 310,000, and nearly 50,000 were Irish. In this ten-year period, the Irish population in Boston had increased from one-fiftieth to one-sixth.

Now, there had never been any love lost between the British and the Irish back in the old country. It was certainly no different in the new. Families from good English stock thought of themselves as an American form of aristocracy. They didn't want to share their jobs and neighborhoods with any lower class "micks." One of Boston's aristocratic leaders said of the Irish: "They were the scum of creation, beaten men from beaten races, representing the worst failure in the struggle for existence . . . These immigrants were inferior peoples whose prolific issue threatened the very foundations of Anglo-American civilization." Now that got to the root of the problem! The Irish were Catholic!! And wasn't that what the English had left England to escape? It was unthinkable that Catholics should invade this bastion of "purity." And, worst of all, they all had such large families that it would be no time at all before they took over all of Boston!

Yet the Irish were an industrious lot. They would take any job, no matter how menial or humble – as long as it paid something. They worked hard and expected little in return. Anything was better than the poverty they left behind in Ireland. For most of them, a goodly part of their humble wages went to family – parents, brothers and sisters and even wives and children – back home. The dream was always to bring them "out" too.

The New England gentry finally realized that they had a large cheap labor pool at their disposal, as long as they could keep them in their place. They allowed the women (whom they called "Biddy" or "Bridget" regardless of their Christian names) to do the dirty work in their homes. The men generally did hard labor – construction work and road building.

As for housing, the Irish took anything they could find that was cheap. This often meant moving into abandoned neighborhoods, where eight or nine families would share one large house – a family to a room. They would share the one kitchen and the one bathroom. Crowded conditions and lack of proper sanitation often resulted in epidemics of cholera or smallpox.

Nevertheless, the Irish were tough. And they were honest. And they were survivors. And as they started rising above these menial jobs, the "Proper Bostonians" began to worry about the political clout such a large group might have. It was bad enough that they were Catholic, but they were Democrats as well!

To prevent any major changes in their safe little world, the Puritans established residency and literacy laws specifically to exclude the Irish from the voting booth. But, although the Irish had little opportunity for obtaining a formal education either in Ireland or in the new country, they certainly were not dumb. It didn't take them long to learn they could best conquer these laws from within. Once they learned that lesson, politics became the Irish game. They were masters at ward politics, and enjoyed the power it gave them. They beat the Puritans at their own game.

James Michael Curley, an extraordinary fellow by all accounts, typifies the Irish immigrant family who overcame tremendous odds to become powerful in politics. Curley's parents, Sarah Clancy and Michael Curley arrived in Boston aboard different ships in 1864. Sarah was 12 and Michael was 14. They were both healthy and strong, uneducated, poor and ordinary. They had no skills and no discernible talent. Their parents had read the Cunard Line posters in Galway and believed the promise of plentiful jobs, lovely homes and prosperity in New England. They pleaded with every relative, no matter how remote, to give or send them money to come to America.

Ward politics in Boston by the time Michael Curley and his parents arrived, was already firmly established. The ward boss dispensed jobs, helped families make ends meet, took care of wakes and funerals, got people out of jail, and in general acted as intermediary between the people of the ward and the outside world – all in exchange for a vote on election day. Those who beat the drums for the ward boss, or helped in any way, got special attention.

Michael Curley's ward boss got him a job as a hod carrier, but since he was not yet of voting age, ignored him after that. Sarah Clancy did washing, cooking, sewing and other domestic work.

Michael met Sarah when he was 17. They courted for four years and married when he was 21 and she 19. James Michael was the second son, born November 21, 1874. When James Michael was born, his father was working fourteen to sixteen hours a day and earning ten cents an hour.

Michael Curley was an exceptionally large and strong man. He was proud of his brawn. He often boasted that he could lift anything. One day, however, he was challenged to lift a rock that four men had been trying to move. He lifted it alright, but collapsed on the spot. Success killed him! He was thirty-four years old. James Michael was 10.

Sarah Curley took a job scrubbing floors. Her sons worked at whatever they could find. The oldest, John, worked in a grocery store and James Michael, in a drugstore. The combined earnings of the small family barely allowed them to get by – but they did.

James Michael was a shy boy. As he grew older, he was still awkward with women, did not dance or participate in sports or drink. Even when he was 22 years old, he still taught Sunday School and was an usher in church. He was a good conversationalist, though, and an even better listener. And although he had no education beyond grade school, he had been reading a lot. Instead of becoming active in ward politics, he joined the Ancient Order of Hibernians, a club that contained a cross section of Boston Irish. He was active in committee work, selling raffle tickets, raising funds and calling on the sick. Gradually his reputation increased and he was asked to run for office. Although he clearly won his first election, the ward bosses refused to send in the vote. They simply couldn't allow this upstart in their midst when they hadn't even endorsed him.

Losing the election didn't stop Curley, though. By reading the speeches of Gladstone, Disraeli, Burke, Daniel Webster and Lincoln, he learned the art of oratory. He became the finest speaker around. The next time he ran, people listened. And by hiring thugs to block the door of the filing hall, he assured himself a first place position on the ballot. This time he won with no contest. The year was 1899. Boston now had an Irish population of 225,000 – nearly one-half of the city. James Michael Curley was 26. In 1906 he married Mary E. Herlihy. She became his steadying influence and confidant. They had nine children.

Curley was to go on to become a Congressman, Mayor of Boston and Governor of Massachusetts. It wasn't always easy. In fact, he probably lost about as many elections as he won. He is best remembered as the sometimes outrageous and always irrepressible Mayor of his hometown, where he served for 12 years. He was a friend of Roosevelts, Kennedys and Trumans.

Another Boston Irish family of similar background achieved even greater heights. John F. Fitzgerald was eleven years older than Curley, and in many respects, paved the way for Irish politicians who followed him. He was ward boss of the North End and the first American-born son of Irish parents to become mayor of Boston. His daughter Rose was courted by, and married, Joseph P. Kennedy, whose father was ward boss of East Boston.

Now, Joseph Kennedy was not the uneducated man that so many Irish before him were. He had even graduated from

Harvard. Joseph was later to become a millionaire, starting his climb in banking, and was appointed Ambassador to Great Britain under Franklin D. Roosevelt. Few families have given and lost so much for their country. Their son, John Fitzgerald Kennedy was to become the 35th President of the United States, only to be assassinated in 1963. Another son, Robert, was assassinated while running for the presidency in 1968. A third son, Edward (Teddy), has served as U.S. Senator from the state of Massachusetts since 1962.

John F. Kennedy probably best summed up his family's dedication to public service by the following quotation. He was speaking to the Massachusetts State Legislature in January 1961: "For of those to whom much is given, much is required. And when at some future date the high court of history sits in judgment on each of us, recording whether in our brief span of service we fulfilled our responsibilities to the state, our success or failure, in whatever office we hold, will be measured by the answers to four questions: First, were we truly men of courage . . . Second, were we truly men of judgment . . . Third, were we truly men of integrity . . . Finally, were we truly men of dedication?"

Not only has Massachusetts led the nation in politics and learning, but it has also produced some of America's finest artists and writers. The first book printed in the new country was at Harvard, probably on that printing press acquired by Harvard's first president, Henry Dunster, when he married the rich widow Glover. "The Bay Book of Psalms" was written by a committee of ministers so that their congregations could sing the Psalms on Sundays. It was a bestseller for years.

More books followed. Booksellers even had books imported from England and France. By 1700, there were 20 bookstores in Boston. New York, by comparison, had only four. Benjamin Franklin's "Poor Richard's Almanac" contained his witty proverbs and satires of British policies in America and was found in most New England homes.

In the early 1800s, literature in New England truly flowered. Edgar Allen Poe, born in Boston in 1809, wrote the first detective stories. One of the most influential writers was Ralph Waldo Emerson who started the Transcendental Movement. It was his belief that independent thought was the salvation of mankind and that a return to nature insured clean, pure thought. He said: "A foolish consistency is the hobgoblin of little minds, adored by little statesmen and philosophers and divines. With consistency a great soul has simply nothing to do . . . Speak what you think today in hard words and tomorrow speak what tomorrow thinks in hard words again, though it contradict everything you said today."

Some undoubtedly thought that was a bunch of foolishness. But not Henry David Thoreau, who built a cabin in the woods on Walden Pond (near Boston), lived there for two years, and wrote about it. Neither did Nathaniel Hawthorne nor Amos Bronson Alcott. They founded a community near Concord, Massachusetts, called Brook Farm – an experiment in communal living with simplicity as its core. This is where Alcott's daughter, Louisa May, wrote an account of her childhood called "Little Women."

Other writers, including Harriet Beecher Stowe and Mark Twain, formed a community near Hartford, Connecticut, called Nook Farm. It was in a pastoral woodland setting beside the north branch of the Park River. All the homes were comfortable Victorian dwellings with lacy gingerbread decoration. Several of these are now open to the public. Although Mrs. Stowe wrote "Uncle Tom's Cabin" in Brunswick, Maine, while her husband was a teacher at Bowdoin College, her simple Victorian cottage is a delight to visit.

To visit the home of Mark Twain, one of America's most beloved and famous writers, is to step back in time and take the tour with him. His house, built in 1874, is a whimsical stick-style Victorian with open porches, balconies, towers and decorative brick work. It looks as high-spirited and individualistic as he must have been. He is reputed to have smoked forty cigars a day and to have slept backwards in his bed. Why? He wanted to face his elaborately carved Victorian headboard. His billiard room is where he did his best writing. This gregarious man loved to entertain and often had Rudyard Kipling or General Sherman over. He was intrigued by the latest inventions and had the first private telephone in Hartford. It was in this house that he wrote "The Adventures of Tom Sawyer" and "The Adventures of Huckleberry Finn." Inside the house he built a dressing room that looks like the wheelhouse of a Mississippi riverboat to remind him of his days as a river pilot. The interior also includes ornately carved woodwork, silver stenciling and special wall coverings.

Mark Twain was not really Mark Twain at all, but Samuel Clemens. He described his choice of names: "I was a fresh, new journalist, and needed a nom de guerre; so I confiscated the ancient mariner's discarded one, and have done my best to make it remain what it was in his hands – a sign and symbol and warrant that whatever is found in its company may be gambled on as being the petrified truth." Some of Mark Twain's homilies are favorites of American literature:

"Why is it that we rejoice at a birth and grieve at a funeral? It is because we are not the person involved."

"Grief can take care of itself, but to get the full value of a joy you must have somebody to divide it with."

"Always do right. This will gratify some people, and astonish the rest."

"Familiarity breeds contempt – and children."

Of all New England's writers, perhaps the best, and the one who has given most back to America, is Henry Wadsworth Longfellow. Longfellow was born in Portland, Maine in 1807. He attended Bowdoin College in Brunswick, Maine, and then became a professor of modern languages at Harvard. His simple narrative poems about America's folk heroes, make him the American Shakespeare. He wrote about Hiawatha and Evangeline, Miles Standish and Paul Revere and about patriotism and rural life. Perhaps one of the best examples is found in "The Village Blacksmith," where he wove a portrait of rural American life mixed with the Puritan idea that hard work and toil are their own reward:

"Under a spreading chestnut-tree
  The village smithy stands; . . .
His brow is wet with honest sweat,
  He earns whate'er he can,
And looks the whole world in the face,
  For he owes not any man . . .

Toiling, – rejoicing, – sorrowing,
  Onward through life he goes;
Each morning sees some task begin,
  Each evening sees its close;
Something attempted, something done,
  Has earned a night's repose . . ."

Literature wasn't the only art that New England excelled in. Artists flourished as well. The first genuine American painter was John Smibert, who set up a studio in Boston in 1729. One of his pupils, John Singleton Copley became America's first important portraitist. Copley painted such leading citizens as Paul Revere. He painted in a precise, exact, life-like fashion and exhibited a keen attention to detail and to surface texture.

Benjamin West, born in Springfield, Massachusetts in 1738, travelled to London to study and became a leader of the Neo-Classical movement. His students included Samuel F. B. Morse, who was an exceptionally fine portraitist before he became an inventor (one of his inventions was the telegraph) and John Trumbull, the son of the governor of Connecticut. John Trumbull was an aide-de-camp to General Washington during the Revolutionary War. He kept a sketchbook as his constant companion. His sketches of the Signing of the Declaration of Independence, The Resignation of General Washington, The Surrender of General Burgoyne at Saratoga and The Surrender of Lord Cornwallis at Yorktown, were later commissioned as paintings and decorate the rotunda of the Capitol in Washington D.C. It's his exceptional detailing including likenesses of the participants at each event that make his paintings so historically accurate.

New England was home to other renowned American artists as well, including James McNeill Whistler, who was born in Lowell, Massachusetts, in 1834, Winslow Homer who painted his large canvases of the sea for many summers in Prout's Neck, Maine, and Norman Rockwell, whose covers for the Saturday Evening Post are beloved essays on American life. He did many of his paintings in his adopted village of Stockbridge, Massachusetts. He would use the local druggist, 8 year old Sara Jane on her way home from school, or the firestation's pet dog as models. His paintings are filled with a sense of humor and a keen eye to common every-day events of American life. He made us all see a bit of ourselves reflected in his drawings.

It must be the good clean New England air, or the indomitableness of the Puritan spirit, or the peacefulness of a quiet New England town that created some of those great American artists. It was probably a pinch of all three that gave us Anna Mary Robertson (Grandma) Moses. This plucky little lady started painting in her native village of Bennington, Vermont in the 1930s when she was 70 years old. She painted scenes of the rural countryside and farm life in a simple folk manner. She won her first show in the 1940s, was received by President Truman when she was 90 and continued to paint until her death at 101. A museum to her work is housed in the little schoolhouse she attended as a girl.

History doesn't record whether Grandma Moses ever visited New Bedford or not, but if she didn't, she surely must have wanted to. New where? New Bedford is a charming city tucked away in the southeast corner of Massachusetts, right on Buzzards Bay, just off Rhode Island sound. Shipping and whaling built this town. In fact, a salty atmosphere still pervades the cobblestone streets that lead down to the waterfront.

In 1765 Joseph Rotch moved to New Bedford from Nantucket. He had been "into" whaling on Nantucket, but Nantucket's harbor was too shallow for the newest ships. So he decided to establish a whaling industry in New Bedford. Within ten years there were 50 three-masted whaling ships that berthed in New Bedford and by the 1830s it was the whaling capital of the world. During the peak of New Bedford's prosperity – about 1857 – there were over 330 ships valued at $12 million, and more than 10,000 men involved in the whaling industry.

Whale oil was used to light the homes and streets of cities across America and Europe. Whalebone was used for corset stays, umbrellas and walking sticks. Whale spermaceti was used to make fine-smelling candles. New Bedford and the other whaling centers were a beehive of activity. It was not an uncommon sight to see thousands of barrels of whale oil, recently unloaded from ships, stored along the wharves.

Shipbuilding became an important activity and the quest for ever sturdier and safer ocean-going vessels was unending. New England-built whaling ships plied the waters from Greenland to the North Pacific, from the Azores to Brazil and from Polynesia to Japan. It was not unusual for a voyage to last up to five years. Whole families would often accompany the captain, but life aboard a whaler was difficult. There were few comforts and the food was poor. It was dangerous too. A whale could capsize a whaling boat and often did.

The crew of a whaling ship generally numbered from 15 to 20 men. Months could go by without seeing a whale, but when one was spotted, the activity became frantic. There was always a sailor on watch and as soon as he would spot the fine mist a whale exhales when breathing, he would shout "Thar she blo-o-ows!" With that, a small whaling boat would be lowered into the water and a crew of 6 to 8 would row toward the whale. When they got close enough, they would harpoon it and that was when the fun began because no one knew what the whale was going to do. It might dive below the surface, or it might attack the boat, or it might race away, pulling the little whaling boat along at speeds up to 20 miles an hour. The men called that a Nantucket sleigh ride. Once the whale tired sufficiently, they would kill it and take it back to the ship. That's where they would clean and process it.

The entire whaling industry declined after petroleum was discovered in Pennsylvania, but it was really the Civil War and some bad breaks that dealt the final blow to New Bedford's whaling fleet. About 35 whaling vessels were destroyed by the Confederate ship Shenandoah in 1865, and then several dozen others were lost in the "Stone Fleet" episode. It was called the "Stone Fleet" because, to prevent blockade runners from entering Charlestown, whaling ships were loaded with stone and sunk in the harbor. Then in 1861, an additional 32 ships were abandoned in the Arctic Ocean when they became icebound. That tragedy was repeated in 1876, 1888 and 1897. After that there wasn't much of the fleet left.

New Bedford's whaling industry is preserved in its marvelous Whaling Museum, and its illustrious past is described wonderfully in Herman Melville's classic novel "Moby Dick." The wealth and prosperity that whaling brought to New Bedford can still be glimpsed in its stately mansions. In 1840 Melville described New Bedford: "All those brave houses and flowery gardens came from the Atlantic, Pacific and Indian Oceans, one and all they were harpooned and dragged up hither from the bottom of the sea."

From New Bedford it's an easy hop skip and jump to Cape Cod, Nantucket and Martha's Vineyard.

Cape Cod was founded even before the first settlers arrived on the Mayflower. The explorer Bartholomew Gosnold landed on the Cape in 1602. He was so impressed by the numerous cod he found swimming in the waters that he named it Cape Cod. Fishing and farming have always been the principal occupations. Speaking of farming, over half of the nation's cranberries are grown in southern Massachusetts, many on Cape Cod.

Cape Cod is actually an island now, but it wasn't always so. To make it easier for boats to go from Boston to Newport, a canal was dug right at the neck connecting Cape Cod Bay and Buzzards Bay. They may have made it easier for boats, but it's certainly more difficult for people. On a nice summer day the traffic can be blocked for hours waiting to cross one of the two bridges.

Cape Cod is principally a tourist haven in summer. Its more than 40 miles of lovely sandy beaches are the draw. Sad to say, the proliferation of fast food stands, motels and shopping centers that line most of Route 28 along the south shore, makes one forget how charming it must have been at one time. The Cape Cod National Seashore thankfully does preserve a 27,000 acre stretch of the shore from Nauset out to Provincetown. Provincetown, way out on the tip, is an old fishing port that is now an artist's colony, resort and fishing village.

Provincetown gained recognition as an artist's colony in the early 20th century when such prominent Broadway playwrights as Sinclair Lewis and Tennessee Williams fled Broadway in protest over its rigid rules. They settled in Provincetown and produced plays that were quite experimental for their time. Eugene O'Neill's career began in Provincetown. His first play, "Bound East for Cardiff" was produced here and was a huge success. Many of his plays were set in New England, including "Desire Under the Elms," "Beyond the Horizon" and "Mourning Becomes Electra."

It was, in fact, one of Eugene O'Neill's plays that launched another equally famous, but quite different career. Howard Johnson is a typical New Englander. He was born in Boston and raised in a strict New England family, where the old Yankee ideal of hard work and no play were the measure of success. He never graduated from high school, insisting instead on going to work in his father's cigar business. One summer he worked out a deal to be paid on a commission plus expenses basis. He bought a Stutz Bearcat and started burning up the New England roads. He racked up a commission of $25,000 in one year. His father settled by paying him $4,000. He thought $25,000 was just too much for a young man to make. When his father died unexpectedly, Howard inherited the cigar business, but it was bankrupt!

Howard tried to make a go of the cigar business, but his manufacturers in Puerto Rico were not always making the cigars up to snuff and business declined. One day he passed a run down store opposite the Wollaston (a Boston suburb) railroad station. He bought it and started making special sodas. He had this idea that if you put the scoop of ice cream in the soda last, and the syrup and fizz ran down the sides of the glass, people would think they were getting a bargain, even at a higher price. And they did. Business kept steadily improving.

Then, when a local ice cream peddler decided to retire, Johnson bought his ice cream recipe. Everyone had loved that Peddler's ice cream! What Johnson found, was that the peddler had the best ice cream around because he had been using twice as much butterfat as anyone else. Johnson started doing the same and business got even better. In the summers, Johnson ran ice cream stands at the beach.

Next he expanded to a larger restaurant. And that's where Eugene O'Neill came in. The restaurant was near the Quincy Theatre. O'Neill's play "Strange Interlude" had been banned in Boston, so it opened in Quincy. It was a long play and had an hour and one-half intermission. The theatre was packed every night and they crowded into Johnson's restaurant for dinner. He had a gold mine. The only problem was that when the play closed, his business plummeted. There he was, left with a restaurant and no customers. His first attempt at fine dining failed and he was left with huge debts.

Now Johnson always seemed to have another scheme up his sleeve and debt never bothered him much. His attitude toward debt was that if you let your creditors know your financial picture, then they would understand if you didn't get the payment to them on time. He sent all of them his accountant's report. "If you are in debt to a man," Johnson once said, "you owe it to him to let him know exactly how your business stands. And when he knows you aren't holding anything back, he isn't going to be hard on you if occasionally you can't pay a bill the day it falls due."

He still had all his ice cream stands – a dozen by now – and eventually acquired a few restaurants of his own. One day he was approached by a friend who had some property on a well-travelled highway on Cape Cod to sell. He thought it would be a great place for a restaurant. They talked it over and decided that not only was it a good place, but that the friend would run it.

Johnson put up some money and they signed a contract that the restaurant would sell Howard Johnson ice cream exclusively and buy other Johnson products such as candies, fountain syrups, preserved fruits. Johnson also hired the help, gave the man lessons in how to run a restaurant and required that the restaurant maintain certain high standards. Other than that, the new entrepreneur was on his own. They called it Howard Johnson's to capitalize on the Johnson name. And to make it typically New England, they served such specialities as Boston baked beans and brown bread.

The restaurant was a tremendous success and more and more franchises followed. The white colonial-style buildings with orange roof and blue-green shutters became a familiar sight on America's roads and a sure sign of quality. The Howard Johnson formula reaped success after success. There are now 805 Howard Johnson restaurants up and down the East Coast and across the continent. But that doesn't include that first franchise in Orleans on Cape Cod. That's closed now – perhaps unable to withstand the competition from all the McDonald's, Kentucky Fried Chicken and Skippers Fish and Chips that it spawned.

So, if quaint villages are the quest on Cape Cod, a drive along route 6A on the north shore – the Cape Cod Bay side – is sure to please. The villages of Barnstable, Yarmouth and Dennis are small and charming. Best of all though, are the museums and outstanding antique shops, often located in old mansions, amid spacious lawns, well off the highway. Some of the Cape's best eating establishments are in similar settings.

Cape Cod is also the best way to reach two of nature's finest works: Nantucket and Martha's Vineyard. Both are accessible by boat from Hyannis. Nantucket lies 30 miles offshore. The name is an Indian one that means "distant land." It's a very special place that time seems to have forgotten.

Nantucket reigned as the world capital of the whaling industry for over 100 years, before New Bedford even knew what whalers were. But New Bedford had a deeper port and as ships grew larger, Nantucket just couldn't compete. Nevertheless Nantucket merchants and shipowners grew very rich by selling whale oil all over the world. They built grand homes that still remain on Main Street.

Nantucket homes often have a small fenced platform on the very top that provides an excellent unobstructed view of the ocean. It's called a "widow's walk" and it just may have been the idea of a Nantucket housewife. When her husband's ship set sail for a voyage of several years, she could run up to her "widow's walk" to wave a last goodbye. Periodically, as his return drew nearer, she would go back up to catch the first sight of his return. "Widow's walks" are found on homes in seaside towns throughout New England.

And once the seafaring captains did return, Nantucketers devised a sure sign of welcome. When the captains made their trips all over the world in search of whales, they often stopped in various ports of call and bought delicacies to bring home with them. Pineapples were especially popular. Everyone loved their sweet-sharp taste. To let the whole town know that the captain had returned from a voyage, and would love to have visitors stop in to say hello, it became the custom to stick a pineapple on one of the sharp wrought iron posts just beside the gate. The neighbors would troop in to welcome him home and to take away a few pineapples with them. Eventually the pineapples were made of wrought iron and included in the design of the gate and fence. From that day to this, pineapples have been the symbol of hospitality and welcome. Some can still be seen all over New England and as far away as Virginia and Greenwich village in New York.

Nantucket is worth every bit of the trouble it takes to get there. And the trip by boat is a relaxing start to enjoying a relaxed way of life. Nantucket didn't receive her nickname "The little grey lady in the sea" for nothing. It's filled with cottages weathered grey by the salt air. They're all wrapped up with white trim and shutters and covered with pink roses in the summer. The cobblestone streets and salty wharfside structures are filled with antique shops and restaurants where seafood is the speciality. A meal of tiny, fragrant and oh-so-tender Nantucket Bay scallops is pure heaven.

In springtime, the daffodils come out and, in celebration, Nantucketers hold a Daffodil Festival. It's usually toward the end of April when the golden flowers spill out of window boxes, flower pots and gardens. April is the time of year when Nantucket is blessed with another phenomenon too. Those tasty little fish, the herring, cause considerable excitement each year when they return to their freshwater spawning grounds in Long Pond.

Martha's Vineyard is another story altogether. On that same trip when Bartholomew Gosnold found Cape Cod, he also landed on "The Vineyard." Here he found wild grapes growing in profusion and named the island for the grapes and for his young daughter, Martha. The towns on Martha's Vineyard are small fishing villages and summer resorts, each with a character of its own.

The villages of Oak Bluffs and Edgartown are filled with gingerbread Victorian dwellings, each of them very distinctive. None of that catalog-ordered trim for these folks! Their carpenters used originality and imagination to create some of the most extravagant examples of Victorian architecture to be found anywhere.

Northern Massachusetts has a charm all its own, but quite different from Cape Cod and the islands. Salem offers much to interest the traveler, even if witches went out of fashion long ago. Because of its natural harbor and its accessibility to the ocean, Salem became the shipbuilding capital of the colonies. During the revolution, Salem ships raided and captured about 400 British ships. After the revolution was over, they kept going further and further afield and eventually established worldwide trade routes, especially to China.

The China Trade was developed by boats sailing from the East Coast to the Far East. But this was before the Panama Canal, so they had to sail around the tip of South America. The voyage around the "horn" was a most treacherous one. The captains would make several detours to obtain goods that could be used in China to barter for silks, porcelains and tea. Furs, for example, were acquired in the Pacific Northwest, sandalwood in the Sandwich Islands etc. Later, the boats went to India and Turkey to barter for opium before going to China. Opium always brought a high price.

Canton was the only Chinese port open to foreign trade. But foreign merchants weren't allowed within the city. Ships would drop anchor about 10 miles outside Canton and the merchants would continue upriver in small boats to the quarters built to house them. The search for the luxuries craved by folks back home would last several months. Once the luxurious silks, tea, decorative art and pictures were obtained, the ships would set sail for home. Along the way they might stop in Sumatra for pepper, Java for sugar and coffee, Bombay and Madras for cotton, Zanzibar for ivory and Ceylon for spices.

The wealthy businessmen of Salem and Boston would place orders with their friends in the shipping business to bring something very special back for their wives. One item that was especially popular was a silk shawl, heavily fringed all around and embroidered with a fine silk thread in exquisite detail. These shawls were painstakingly embroidered by hand in an all-over floral design. They often measured as much as five feet square. It became a common sight to see women promenading on a summer evening with one of these beautiful shawls around their shoulders. It was even more common to drape a shawl over the most prominent table in the house – maybe the dining room or a hall table – so that it was the first thing a visitor would see on entering. Perhaps there would even be a shiny black Cantonese lacquer box inlaid with ivory on top. If so, it would certainly have the lid tilted open on the table to reveal the intricately detailed contents of a sewing box. Ivory pin boxes, thimbles, carved boxes for needles or buttons and minutely carved thread holders were all arrayed on exquisite silk brocade, to be exclaimed over. It is doubtful that these boxes were ever used for sewing.

With all these ships in Salem (and Boston too) the owners were always looking for ways to keep them busy.

So, another ingenious and original industry was developed in the 19th century. Ice was often seen floating in big chunks off the Maine seacoast and north off Nova Scotia. With all that ice around someone reasoned that they just might be able to harvest it for profit. They were always looking for an opportunity, those New Englanders. So, in winter, they went to an ice field, removed the snow by oxen and sawed the ice into blocks. It was then packed in sawdust and stored in ice houses until spring, when the ice on the river had thawed enough to allow a ship to harbor. The ice was then loaded into specially designed ships and taken to the southern states or to the West Indies or even as far away as Calcutta. And, sure enough, another profitable business prospered – until someone invented the refrigerator.

It was just this same sort of ingenuity, and ice, that made Clarence Birdseye rich and famous. Clarence was a New

Englander, too. He was raised in Gloucester, Massachusetts. But it was while he was fur trading in Labrador in 1915 that Birdseye got his idea. One day while he was fishing through a hole in the ice at 65° below zero, he noticed how the fish he caught froze the instant he pulled them from the water. When they were thawed out, they were as firm and juicy as if they had been caught that same day.

Now folks had been freezing fish for some time, but generally they were soggy, mushy and inedible when they were thawed. So, Birdseye started quick freezing fish and meats and vegetables that were almost as good as fresh. And he made it possible for people in Kansas to eat good fish from Maine, and people in Maine to eat good beef from Kansas, and everyone to eat corn in the spring.

New Englanders were becoming pretty sophisticated folk by this time, especially along the seacoast. Inland, however, life remained much the same for the farmers who worked their plots of land. A trip across Massachusetts, even today, will reveal a rural life that has changed little over the years.

The lovely Berkshire mountains in western Massachusetts are a good example. In fall, this is a favorite spot to view that wonderful phenomenon of nature that turns the green leaves to brilliant shades of red, orange, yellow and rust.

What causes the trees to change their clothes every year? Indian summers mean that crisp, clear, sunny days are followed by longer and colder nights. This brings about a halt in the production of cholorphyll in the leaves and causes them to turn color and eventually to fall off. It's the birches, poplars and gingkos that turn vivid gold, the maples, hickories and mountain-ash that become orange and the maples, red oak, sassafras and dogwoods, that turn scarlet. Add to this the soft shades of green in the meadows and a backdrop of dark evergreen trees, and it's pure magic.

But fall is not the only time of year set aside for visiting The Berkshires. It's lovely all times of year. Wind down pretty little country lanes, with trees so thick they form a canopy, turn a corner and see a green field surrounded by a split rail fence or a pasture of very contented cows. Make yet another turn and there's a white country church with steeple and bell tower and a red door. This is The Berkshires.

Nathaniel Hawthorne and Henry Ward Beecher knew The Berkshires well. They wrote about its beauty frequently. That attracted other wealthy families to summer there. They built handsome estates. At the beginning of the 20th century Lenox alone had 75 of these magnificent properties,

including that of Andrew Carnegie, who was undoubtedly the wealthiest. Some of these estates are used now as inns or restaurants or schools but others are still used as summer residences.

Two of the most interesting of these estates are now open to the public. Tanglewood was the residence of the Tappan family and the estate contains a replica of the cottage where Nathaniel Hawthorne lived for 18 months and wrote "House of Seven Gables." But this estate is much more famous as the home of the Berkshire Music Festival every summer. This festival was started in 1934 with concerts given by the New York Philharmonic, but since 1936 it's been the summer home of the Boston Symphony Orchestra. The festival attracts over 250,000 people every summer, and no wonder!

The setting is wonderful, with a 6,000 seat shed, open on three sides, as the focal point. It's in this shed that the stage is located. But, for those in the know, the place to listen from is on the spacious lawns that surround it. People start arriving mid-afternoon for the evening concerts. They bring blankets, folding chairs and even chaise lounges. But that's only the beginning. For a country that loves to picnic, Tanglewood is the ultimate. It's an excuse to bring out all the picnic gear and the recipes that have been handed down from grandma. Boston baked beans, potato salad, cole slaw, fried chicken, corn, home baked breads and cakes and cookies are all washed down with wine or beer. For gala festive concerts, it's not unusual to see caterers bringing oriental carpets and pillows for guests to sit on. Silver candelabra with tapered candles are lighted and an elaborate array of foods come in six or seven courses. Some guests for these events arrive in black tie and long dresses and have reserved seats in the shed for the concert. But for the average music lover, to have a good meal and then lie back on the grass and allow Mozart's overture to "Cosi Fan Tutte" to wash over him, is pure ecstasy.

The music at Tanglewood is the best part and the variety is unending. Recitals are often given in the afternoons and in the evenings the Boston Symphony Orchestra is often joined by the Tanglewood Festival Chorus. The Boston Pops always make several appearances and some of the world's most famous conductors, such as Leonard Bernstein and Andre Previn, are invited to conduct. In addition to the Music Festival, the Berkshire Playhouse in Stockbridge offers summer theatre and the Jacob's Pillow Dance Festival offers programs of ballet, modern dance and mime.

The charming Berkshire village of Stockbridge is home to the Old Corner House, a museum that displays some of Norman Rockwell's most famous illustrations, and to the Red

Lion Inn, an old style country inn, filled with antiques, that fronts on Main Street. One can sit in the comfortable wicker chairs on the wide front porch and look out on a Main Street that has remained unchanged for a century. And down the street, the small railroad station was designed by Stanford White.

Stockbridge was also home to Daniel Chester French, one of America's most famous sculptors. His estate is open to the public as a National Trust property. French is best remembered for his sculpture of "Seated Lincoln" for the Lincoln Memorial in Washington, D.C. But in his lifetime from 1850 to 1931, he actually executed over 1000 statues. He achieved his first major success at the tender age of 21 with his statue of the "Minute Man" honoring the patriots who resisted the British at Concord. It stands at the Old North Bridge in the Minuteman National Historical Park in Concord.

Now it's certainly true that not all of New England, or even Massachusetts, has the bucolic grace and charm of the Berkshires. Another quite different side of Massachusetts is found in the mill towns that sprang up in the early 19th century. Lowell is a good example. In 1817, Frances Cabot Lowell, who had developed the power loom in America, selected a site on the Merrimack River for a planned community. Water power was the energy source that would operate his mills. Although he died before he could finish the project, a group of Boston investors did. They built a mill town of red brick factories, warehouses, stores and houses – and everything was company-owned. Lowell became the world leader in textile production.

Success was simplicity itself. There was a plentiful supply of cotton in the south. Water power was abundant and cheap in New England and a steady, cheap supply of labor was arriving in Boston daily. How could the plan fail?

The workers were mainly young women who worked from five in the morning to seven in the evening. Their housing consisted of a room shared with as many as six other girls. They lived in a boarding house run by operators selected by the mill owners. Room and board were deducted from the girl's meager pay. Curfew was at ten o'clock every night and *everyone* was required to go to church, where the minister undoubtedly preached about the virtues of duty, obedience and hard work.

Everything was grand for the mill towns until the stock market crash of 1929. But after that, the textile companies moved south and the mill towns of New England "dried up."

Factories and warehouses, that had once been the scene of bustling activity, were boarded up and the slow process of deterioration began. Only a few, like Lowell, have regained some of their former prominence. Lowell is once again a manufacturing center. Sections of it were declared a National Park in 1978 and an extensive restoration program is going on.

Some of the folks who left Lowell and the mill towns like it went "out West" to places like Ohio and Illinois. They often took their concept of what a small town should be, with its trees, common and church, along with them. In fact, they took their missionary zeal as well. Horrified to find that everyone didn't attend church on Sundays, they took it upon themselves to bring religion to the heathen.

Sometimes this zeal made them appear to be putting on airs, or displaying a sense of superiority that was not fully appreciated. An anonymous note in "View of the Valley of the Mississippi," certainly made the local's opinion of this attitude clear: "The eastern emigrant will find warm-hearted friends in every neighborhood in this state. The people of the West have much plain and blunt, but sincere hospitality. And any emigrant who comes among them with a disposition to be pleased with the country and its inhabitants, – to partake of their hospitality cheerfully – to make no invidious comparisons, – to assume no airs of distinction, – and in a word, to feel at home in this region, where, of course, everything is very different from what he has been accustomed to, will be truly welcome. Fastidious and reserved manners, a disposition to be forever unfavourably contrasting the West with the East, – and to find fault with everything around him, – will speedily render any emigrant an object of dislike and neglect." Let that be a warning!!

It was to a New Englander that Horace Greeley, editor of the New York Tribune, addressed his famous remark: "The best business you can go into you will find on your father's farm or in his workshop. If you have no family or friends to aid you, and no prospect opened to you there, turn your face to the great West, and there build up a home and fortune." This has been freely translated into: "Go West, young man, go West."

The man he directed this advice to was Josiah Grinnell. Greeley must have liked this young man a lot because he followed up the advice with an assignment to report on the 1853 Illinois State Fair for the Tribune. After the assignment was completed, Grinnell continued on out to Ohio where he founded the town of Grinnell, as well as Grinnell College.

Josiah Grinnell knew where he was going, but that wasn't

always the case. Way back in the late 18th century, a little group of Connecticut folk had heard that the fields were more fertile and the grass greener out West. They decided to find out for themselves and after travelling day and night, reached a spot that suited them perfectly. It was green and lush and exactly what they had been told Western Connecticut looked like. They praised the Lord for leading them to this promised land and settled down to raise some corn.

Meanwhile, another group with the same thought in mind was travelling north from Philadelphia. They arrived in the same valley, looked at their maps and said "Here we are in Northern Pennsylvania." But what were these other folks doing here?

As it turned out, Connecticut's grant had no western boundary and Pennsylvania's had no northern one. It took three wars and a lot of verbal confrontations leading up to them, to settle that dispute. And it was the king who goofed. He was so far away, what did he know anyway?

Connecticut has often been described as the promised land. As early as 1633, the Dutch were impressed by the navigability of the Connecticut River and established a trading post where Hartford is today. It was called Fort Good Hope. They mostly traded furs and timber, but when folks started fleeing the tyranny and strict puritanism of the Massachusetts Colony, they settled on the Connecticut River to farm its fertile valleys.

By 1638 Hartford was flourishing, so to form a "body politik" like its Massachusetts neighbors, it joined with the tiny villages of Windsor and Wethersfield to form the Hartford Colony. They drew up a document called the Fundamental Orders of Connecticut. This document has been called a model of democracy and is the example on which the United States Constitution is based. In reality, however, Connecticut's government was scarcely more democratic than Massachusetts. They based suffrage (the right to vote) on property instead of religious qualifications, but that simply meant that the wealthy could vote whether they were "pure" or not. In 1662, The Hartford Colony became the Colony of Connecticut, with its independence guaranteed by a Royal Charter from the King.

But then an odd thing happened. For some reason, the King's representative, the Royal Governor Edmond Andros, asked for the charter back. The colonists and the governor met to discuss it, but in the midst of the discussion, someone blew out the candle and ran off with the charter. The colonists knew it was hidden in an old oak tree, but the governor didn't. He finally returned to England without the charter. Years later, the oak (known by now as the Charter Oak) was felled in a storm. By that time, of course, the charter had been removed, but the oak was a legend. Everything imaginable was claimed to have been made from that old oak tree. Mark Twain once remarked that there were "…a walking stick, dog collar, needle case, three-legged stool, bootjack, dinner table, tenpin alley, toothpicks and enough Charter Oak to build a plank road from Hartford to Salt Lake City."

Hartford's prominence as the "Insurance Capital of the Nation" started off inauspiciously enough. It certainly wasn't the first place to offer fire insurance. That honor goes to Philadelphia, thanks to Benjamin Franklin. In fact, New York City had more insurance companies and insured more businesses than Hartford did until an event occurred in 1835. A very bad fire broke out in New York City on October 31st that destroyed over 600 buildings. Many of them were insured by New York insurance companies, and the fire forced them into bankruptcy, so they certainly couldn't pay all those claims. But the Hartford Fire Insurance Company could pay its policyholders. And to assure everyone of that fact, the president came to New York in the midst of a snowstorm to personally tell his clients.

This same story was repeated when similar disasters occurred in Boston and Chicago. The San Francisco earthquake of 1906 cinched it for Hartford. From that time on, Hartford has enjoyed the best reputation of any city in the United States and is the indisputable insurance capital.

It was life insurance that played a key role in shaping current-day New England life too. Factory workers in the mill towns and in the rising industrial centers, worried constantly about how their families would fare if something happened to them. But they certainly didn't have enough money to buy a standard insurance policy. What to do? The insurance companies had an idea and it paid off handsomely. They sold lots and lots more insurance.

What the insurance companies did was to issue policies with a face value of approximately two and one-half times the wage earners annual salary – and devised a payment plan that could be collected on a weekly basis. They then hired a battery of agents, gave them a territory and said: "Go forth and collect." And they did. Often, back in the 1920s, when the plan began, the weekly premium was as small as 3¢. Families found that this kind of payment plan was remarkably painless, and they watched their equity grow. It was a form of forced savings, so as babies were born, they were added to the policy. Pretty soon, the agents were collecting 50¢ – $1.00 a week. And the insurance companies grew richer and richer.

But the best part of this savings plan was the weekly call by the insurance agent. He became an integral part of the family. They all knew what time he would round the bend and would have tea and cookies or his favorite supper dish ready.

James Farnsworth is retired now, but he was an agent for Metropolitan Life Insurance Company from 1932 to 1971. His territory covered Torrington, Thomaston, Terryville and Litchfield in Western Connecticut. He serviced about 350 families. He would carry a receipt book and each family would have one of their own too. When he received the premium, he would initial the two books and that would be it. Except that he would also have a cup of coffee and lots of conversation. He was made to feel a member of the family and his clients looked on his visit as one of the highlights of their week.

Mr. Farnsworth, as with other agents, was always the first one the family called in time of crisis. If there was a domestic dispute, a question about property taxes or if a son got in trouble with the police for shooting out a street lamp with his slingshot, the agent would be the first one called. He was financial advisor, tax accountant and lawyer. The home service agent was the General Practitioner of the insurance business.

Door-to-door selling seems to thrive in America, and especially in Connecticut. Alfred Carl Fuller found that out. He was born in Nova Scotia and spent his youth in Boston, but it was in Hartford that he realized his dream. Actually, for the first few years after his arrival in Boston, nothing seemed to go right. He was fired from one job after another, perhaps as many as 15. Finally, this awkward, quiet and shy man begged a friend who had a small brush manufacturing plant to let him buy brushes at wholesale, and he would then go out and sell them for whatever he could. And thus was born the Fuller Brush Man.

It wasn't all that easy, of course. But Alfred found that he really did have a knack for selling. He soon had to hire other people to help him sell those brushes. And the demand kept growing and growing. Fuller moved to Hartford, Connecticut in 1909 and started manufacturing his own brushes.

And then he hit upon the idea that made his company unique. It was always a problem getting in the front door. So Fuller decided the way to get around that was to offer the housewife a gift. And it worked. The Fuller Brush Man had to

open his case to get out the gift and he obviously couldn't do that standing out on the doorstep, so the lady invited him in. Once he opened his bag and she saw all those handy brushes, how could she refuse to buy? She seldom did.

Another technique that earned Fuller and his men their sterling reputation, was the requirement that they carry a pair of pliers, a hammer and a screwdriver with them at all times. With these tools, the Fuller Brush Man became the housewife's handyman, fixing everything from electric lights to ironing boards. They would even change diapers and transplant bushes! One wonders how they ever found the time. The average dealer serviced up to 2,500 families and made an average of 50 to 60 calls a day. But it paid off. In 1955, they could make as much as $25,000 a year.

The tiny state of Rhode Island certainly had its share of Fuller Brush Men. But with only 1,214 square miles to cover, at least they could concentrate their efforts. Rhode Island isn't named the Ocean State for nothing. Most of the state is either located right on the water, or close enough to depend on it for survival. Newport and Providence are among the nations leading seaports. In fact, Newport carried on a most interesting enterprise in the mid-18th century, that was to make it one of the most prosperous of all New England cities.

Now it was a known fact that New Englanders liked their rum. They liked it so much that they started making it themselves. Why pay to have it imported all the way from England or Jamaica, they reasoned? Rum wasn't hard to make. All you needed was molasses. And once you had molasses, you could ferment and distill it into rum. But molasses is made from sugar cane, and sugar cane just didn't grow in New England. So, those inventive Newporters started a system known as the triangular trade.

They would send their ships to the West Indies where sugar cane was plentiful, buy lots of molasses and bring it back to Newport. There they would make it into rum, load some of it back on a ship and take it to Africa. (They seem to have been partial to New England rum there.) They would then load the ship with slaves from Africa and take them to the West Indies where they would be traded for molasses and then they'd return to New England. New Englanders didn't believe in slavery and certainly wouldn't have brought any slaves back to New England with them, but they grew very wealthy on the slave trade. Their scruples didn't extend that far.

The lovely mansions built by Newport's shipping and sailing magnates in the 1760s were joined by those of wealthy landholders from Georgia and the Carolinas, who came to

Newport in the summer to escape the heat. Newport was the flower of New England by 1775. But then the British came. They occupied Newport during the revolution from 1776-1779, when looting was encouraged and buildings were burned. At the end of the war, Newport lay in ruins.

Nothing much happened in Newport for about a century. But the cool summer breezes and its excellent location at the head of Narragansett Bay, started attracting the wealthy again shortly after the Civil War. The introduction of steamboat travel from New York accelerated the number of vacationers heading for Newport's salty sea breezes. Soon, it became the fashionable summer residence of America's wealthiest families: the Belmonts, the Astors and the Vanderbilts.

They'd all taken the "grand tour" of Europe and had returned with fanciful notions of stately mansions, palaces, chateaux, villas and castles of Kings, lords and princes dancing in their heads. Not to be outdone by their European cousins – for weren't they America's lords and ladies? – They commissioned America's finest architects to build them castles of equal grandeur. They called them "cottages," but nothing could have been further from the truth. They symbolize the fantastic wealth and excesses of a society that just had so much money they couldn't imagine what to do with it all. No expense was spared.

The fashionable season in Newport was a mere six weeks from mid-July to the end of August, so no one thought to put in central heating. These mansions were never intended for year-round living. Think of the money they saved on heating bills! As the summer season approached in New York, and it got hotter and hotter (they didn't have air conditioning then) families would pack their entire households and move to their "cottage." Servants, children and suitcase after bag, made the trek. Several of the servants would have gone on ahead to "open" the house. This involved taking all the boards and shutters off the windows and literally opening the house up to the summer breezes again. They would also take the coverings off the furniture, stoke up the kitchen stove and have a hot meal ready for the arriving family. Every room had a fireplace so if it was still chilly, a fire would be waiting as well. These Newporters didn't live badly at all.

From mid-July on, Bellevue Avenue and Ocean Drive became the setting for elaborate dinner parties, picnics and balls that were noted for their luxury and extravagance. Even the quixotic tastes were accommodated, as they were the time Harry Lehr gave a champagne and caviar dinner party for friends and their pets! He lined everyone up, at his enormous dining room table, and guests, be they human, canine or feline, all ate side by side. History does not record if anyone brought a pet snake or horse!

Many of the Newport mansions are now open to the public. The Breakers is probably the most fabulous. It was built on a secluded promontory overlooking the ocean by Cornelius Vanderbilt II in 1895. One of the leading architects of the day was Richard Morris Hunt and Vanderbilt commissioned him to design a Renaissance Italian palace. Hunt immediately went to Europe so that he could study the originals first hand. The trip was well worthwhile. Not only did he design a marvelous 70-room mansion but he incorporated an elaborate use of French and Italian stone, marble and alabaster. The exterior has a heavy Italian influence with arcades, columns and cornices, overlooking spacious green lawns that lead down to the ocean. Inside, one enters a Great Hall that is more than two stories high. A magnificent marble staircase leads to a columned arcade that looks out over the Great Hall or leads off to the bedrooms.

The sumptuousness of The Breakers is so elaborate, it's almost indescribable. The music room, for example, has magnificent crystal chandeliers and wall sconces and the fluted columns are embellished with gold leaf, as is the elaborately carved, coffered ceiling. The room is filled with exquisite French and Italian furniture. The state dining room is positively baronial. Allegorical paintings cover the ceiling, an enormous marble fireplace anchors one end, rose colored marble Corinthian columns, with gold leaf trim, frame doorways and accentuate corners and crystal chandeliers and wall sconces light the room. Perhaps, of all the rooms in The Breakers, however, the most exquisite is the tiny 18th century reception room. It's all gold and white and blue and was a gift from Marie Antoinette to her goddaughter.

Not to be outdone by his brother, William Vanderbilt built a fabulous mansion too. His is called Marble House because of all the marble he used. In this case, he asked Richard Morris Hunt to use the Petit Trianon at Versailles as his model. It may not be quite as large, but it does rival the Petit Trianon for lavish decor. The Gold Ballroom is probably the most elaborate room in Newport. It has glittering crystal chandeliers and gold mirrors reflecting them, as well as gold pilasters, arches, doorways and panels. This ballroom has been the scene of some of Newport's most fantastic parties. It was here that the debut of Conseulo Vanderbilt was held shortly before her marriage to the ninth Duke of Marlborough. The grand entrance of Marble House is faced with yellow Siena marble and decorated with Gobelin tapestries. A huge and elaborate grille, weighing 10 tons, acts as a screen between the entrance and the hall. The Gothic Room stands in contrast to the glitter of the Gold Ballroom. Its Gothic arches, polished carved wood doors and bookcases, and fantastic carved ceiling, are all in excellent taste.

Newport's mansions should not be missed when visiting New England, but if it's possible to visit only one, that one might well be Hammersmith Farm. Far removed from the opulence of Bellevue Avenue, Hammersmith is located on Ocean Drive. It was built in 1887, about the same time that Bellevue was gaining prominence, but its plain, shingle style exterior, has none of the extravagance. The gardens and grounds were designed by Frederick Law Olmsted, and offer picturesque vistas of Narragansett Bay.

The House is a homey, comfortable, much-loved place where you can imagine an active, happy family spending many relaxed summers. The interior has polished wooden floors, overstuffed chintz sofas and chairs, and a feeling of restrained elegance. Perhaps one of the best reasons to visit Hammersmith, however, is that the estate was owned by Mrs. Hugh Auchincloss, the mother of Jacqueline Kennedy. President and Mrs. Kennedy were married in Newport in 1953 and returned to Hammersmith often. The farm served as the summer White House from 1961-1963.

To obtain the best view of Newport's mansions, and to get a feeling for the grandeur of Newport's oceanside setting, no one should miss a walk along the ocean on Cliff Walk. It's a narrow, three-mile-long, often rocky path that hugs the coastline and wanders across mansion lawns. It affords wonderful vistas of the estates of Salve Regina College, The Breakers, Rosecliff and Marble House. You'll see fishermen casting their lines out to sea. At one point in the 19th century, estate owners attempted to close the path to the public. A court suit resulted, but the judges liked the walk too. They ruled that the "Toilers of the Sea" should retain access, and the path has remained open to the public ever since.

Now the Coggeshalls aren't Vanderbilts and don't profess to be. They probably wouldn't even want to be. But their roots are more firmly planted in Rhode Island soil than the Vanderbilts ever will be. John Coggeshall came to Boston from England in 1632, but ran into that strict Puritan code along with Anne Hutchinson and Roger Williams. With them, he moved to Rhode Island and became the first president of the Providence Plantation.

In spite of John Coggeshall's leadership, the name does not appear often in history books. But it might from now on. In 1978, a young banker from Struthers, Ohio, with the first name of Robert and the same funny last name, decided to see if he could find any of his relatives. He placed a small inquiry in Yankee Magazine, and waited to see what would happen. He was amazed. Almost immediately, he received 100 replies. From that nucleus, he started a newsletter, and bit by bit the idea formed to hold a reunion. The reunion was held July 22, 1982 and at least 700 people showed up. They came from 36 states to learn more about their clansmen. Even the fact that The Breakers now stands on former Coggeshall land didn't dampen their spirits. For Robert Coggeshall of Ohio, the personal reward of finding his own father made the whole tremendous effort worthwhile.

Rhode Island is abut 100 miles from the wild and spectacular coastline of Maine. By clipper ship it took up to three days, when the ocean was the highway. By horseback, it took two to three times that long. Today the 100 miles can be covered by car on the turnpike in no more than three hours. But what a shame that would be!! The *only* way to see the coastline, and in fact all of New England, is to travel the small byways that lead to tiny fishing villages, cranberry bogs, rugged promontories untamed by man and historic cities like Plymouth, where a replica of the "Mayflower" can be toured.

Once reaching Maine, the visitor is awed by the majesty and grandeur of the beautiful coastline scenery. Maine is as large as all five of the other New England states put together. It has 3,500 miles of coastline and inland areas densely covered with forests. It may have been named by fishermen who use the term "the main" to distinguish mainland from offshore islands, although that is uncertain. It's often referred to as "Downeast" and its residents as "Downeasterners." That's because the winds often carry sailing vessels eastward along this section of the coast.

It was really the French that settled this region first. In 1604, Pierre de Guast, Sieur de Monts and Samuel de Champlain established a small settlement on an island in the St. Croix River. From this small start, they set out the next year to establish the Acadian territory.

About the same time, 1607 to be exact, the English were founding the Popham Colony at the mouth of the Kennebec River. Now these two settlements were about 200 miles distant, so they didn't see much of each other and everything was fine until 1635. At that time Charles I of England took it upon himself to give the entire region, including the Massachusetts Colony, to Sir Ferdinand Gorges and appointed him "Lord of New England." For the next 150 years, the English and the French fought over who owned what.

In 1677, the Massachusetts Colony bought out the descendents of Sir Gorges, including Maine. Finally, in 1783, after the American Revolution, the boundary between the United States and Canada was established by the Treaty of Paris, but Maine remained a part of Massachusetts long after the thirteen colonies formed themselves into a United States. It wasn't until 1820 that Maine was granted statehood. That was one of the "compromises" in the Missouri Compromise.

The great debate over slavery was brewing in the United States House of Representatives. Apparently there had always been a gentlemen's agreement that the number of slave states would exactly equal the number of free. But that was hard to maintain. It all started coming apart when both Alabama and Missouri applied for admission to the United States as slave states. Actually, when Illinois came on board in 1818, there were more free than slave states. With Alabama and Missouri, the bias would shift to slavery. The battle lines were drawn. Debate was hot and often violent. Finally, a compromise was reached. If Maine were given admission as a free state, the balance would be reestablished, and tempers could settle down – for a while, at least. And that's what happened.

Timber has always been one of the most important industries to Maine. It's been used as trade, barter and export for years. In the 18th century, Portland, Maine even had its own mast agent to the King. His name was George Tate and his duties included selecting the finest of Maine's trees for the King. All trees taller than 74 feet and at least 24 inches at the base were marked with the Kings sign and they were thereafter the King's personal property. Tate would then ship them to England to be made into masts for the Royal Navy.

Maine's unspoiled beauty is partly due to its rugged terrain and partly due to its many parks. Acadia National Park is located on Mount Desert Island, and it's made up of 38,000 acres. It's got an interesting history too. Until 1604 the island was the summer fishing ground and campground of the Penobscot and Passamaquoddy Indians. But then, de Champlain and de Monts claimed the area for the French. In the late 17th century the governor of Canada gave Mount Desert Island to the Frenchman Antoine de la Mothe Cadillac. He didn't stay there long, but left the next year to found the city of Detroit. It's doubtful he had cars in mind, however.

By the mid-19th century, Mount Desert was becoming a haven for artists and writers. The more they rhapsodized over the Island's natural beauty, the more people came to see for themselves. Soon elegant summer "cottages," to rival the elegance of Newport, were springing up everywhere. Bar Harbor became a bustling summer resort where elegantly clad men and women arrived daily on steamships and special railroad cars. Spacious Victorian hotels provided lodging for guests and summer residents not lucky enough to have their own "cottages" waiting for them.

The Rockefellers, Astors and Vanderbilts all summered in Bar Harbor, each trying to outdo the other. One mansion is reputed to have had a dining room floor with the center on an elevator. The banquet table would descend when one course was finished, only to reappear again completely set for the next course. No mention is made of the content of table conversation when one minute two people are politely remarking about the weather from across a table, only to see it disappear to be replaced by a gaping hole. Unfortunately, most of these grand homes are mere legends today. Bar Harbor was virtually destroyed by fire in 1947.

The twisty curvy highway that leads from Kittery in southern Maine, to Cobscook Bay on the Nova Scotia border, passes by some of the most charming villages in the world. Ogunquit, Camden, Boothbay Harbor and Kennebunkport all deserve special trips, and more than an overnight stay. All have charming inns, that welcome the weary traveler.

Kennebunkport is an especially charming village and the Captain Lord Mansion an especially inviting inn. It's a large, square house painted yellow with white trim, with a vista over rolling green lawns of the ocean. Inside, the public rooms and the spacious bedrooms have been lovingly restored to their Victorian elegance. There are polished wooden floors and fires crackling in the fireplace to ward off the damp chill even in summer. The conviviality of afternoon tea served to the guests encourages each to share their daily adventures. In the evening there are any number of excellent restaurants to choose from.

It's well to remember that this is lobster country. And nowhere does lobster taste as good as it does fresh from the ocean in Maine. A Maine native will tell you that the best and only way to prepare lobster is to boil it. You can see enormous steaming caldrons of boiling lobster outside many roadside Maine Lobster Restaurants. Inside, you're likely to find a homey, plain atmosphere, with red and white checked tablecloths, and the best lobster you'll eat anywhere. If you like lobster, don't pass these roadside stands by just to eat at the fancier white-tablecloth restaurant that's been recommended by the guidebook. Invariably the lobster is better where it's fresh from the ocean to the pot, and fresh from the pot to you.

The little lobster tails that are served with drawn butter in most restaurants across the United States, bear no resemblance to a Maine Lobster. Most often these are Australian lobster tail and not Maine lobster anyway. A Maine lobster will come to the table whole, and in the shell. And to fully enjoy it, it's best to tie a bib around your neck and dig in. A mallet or nutcracker will be provided and should be used liberally. The tender, sweet meat is a treat long to be remembered.

Approximately 75 per cent of the nation's lobsters come from Maine. The colorful buoys floating on the surface of the water mark the place that lobstermen have set their traps. The lobster trap is a wooden contraption with two compartments. The inner one is baited with fish and the outer one has funnels of nylon netting leading into it. The lobster squirms down the funnel to the prized fish at the other end, but once he reaches the inner compartment, he can't get out again.

Way up in the northern reaches of Maine, such as Baxter State Park, Maine is primarily a wildlife sanctuary for deer, moose, bear and beaver. The park is crisscrossed by nature trails, including the scenic northern section of the Appalachian Trail, which leads from the tip of Maine through New Hampshire and Vermont, the western portion of Massachusetts and on into New York, continuing on south from there. It's a tranquil way to see wild unspoiled rivers tumble into waterfalls, placid alpine lakes and hundreds of flowers from rhododendron and laurel to lupine, lady slippers and Jack-in-the-pulpit.

Maine's rugged coastline is unique, but New Hampshire has a lot going for it too. It's punctuated by hundreds of clear mountain lakes with such unlikely Indian names as Ossipee, Sunapee and Winnipesaukee. Lake Winnipesaukee is really not tiny at all, but covers an area of 72 square miles. It has a shoreline of over 300 miles and contains at least 200 tiny islands. Winnipesaukee means "the smile of the Great Spirit" and God certainly did smile when He created Lake Winnipesaukee. It's now a summer resort with sightseeing cruises, as well as boating and canoeing, the popular sports.

Travelling the rest of New Hampshire will reveal covered wooden bridges, wildwood paths through giant forests and excellent ski resorts in the White Mountain Range. From Mount Washington, the highest point in New England, it's possible to see as far as 50 miles away to Montreal, Quebec, on a clear day.

Portsmouth, right on the Piscataqua River across from Maine and on the Atlantic Ocean, is the capital of New Hampshire. It was settled in 1623 by Englishmen who were so impressed by the wild strawberries lining the banks of the river that they called it Strawbery Banke. Several decades later, they renamed it Portsmouth, because it was "the port at the mouth of the river." Now that's originality for you!

New Hampshire is certainly not without its famous residents either. Perhaps one of the most acclaimed is Augustus Saint-Gaudens, who was America's most famous sculptor in the 19th century. As a young boy he was apprenticed to a cameo cutter, but later studied in Rome and at the Ecole des Beaux Arts in Paris. When he returned from Europe, he established himself in New York, where he often joined with Stanford White and Louis Comfort Tiffany to design some of America's finest buildings. About 150 of the artists sculptures can be seen in the home and studio he maintained for two decades in Cornish, New Hampshire, just across the Connecticut River from Windsor, Vermont.

Literature, art and beauty abound in New England, but so do places of solitude and recreation. Take Vermont, for example. Vermont has always exhibited a head-strong sense of independence. In 1777, Vermont declared itself independent from the rest of the colonial states. They drew up their own constitution outlawing slavery and declaring that property ownership and personal wealth were no longer criteria for voting. Besides that, due to a dispute with New York over land claims, Vermont had been denied admission to the Union. So, for 14 years, they had their own postal service, coined their own money and naturalized citizens of other states. Finally, in 1791, the differences were resolved, and Vermont was granted admission as the 14th state. It really didn't make much difference to them one way or another, though. They continued to function then, as now, just as independently as they always had.

Agriculture is still the biggest industry, with dairy farms dominating the economy. Vermont cheddar cheese is prized for its sharp, pungent taste. Maple syrup is perhaps the oddest of all products. In the early spring when the sap starts to run in the maple trees, and the snow is still on the ground, farmers tap the trees with a spout, allow the sap to drip into a bucket and take it to the small wooden sugarhouse nearby. There they will have a fire going and use evaporators to boil the sap down into sugar. Nothing tastes quite so good as a Vermont breakfast of pancakes loaded with good fresh Vermont butter and covered with pure maple syrup.

Skiing is, without question, the predominant occupation in Vermont in winter. Such famous ski resorts as Stowe,

Killington, Stratton Mountain, Bromley and Sugarbush are ideal for the novice, as well as the experienced skier. The Trapp Family, made famous by the play "The Sound of Music," opened a lodge and ski resort in Stowe, saying it reminded them of their native Austria.

As in all of New England, few settings can quite equal the countryside in fall. That's when the maple, birch, hickory, oak and ash trees become a fiery blaze of reds, oranges, yellows, and gold. In Vermont it's a time for craft fairs, church bazaars, harvest suppers, flea markets and auctions. In Danbury, the Great Danbury State Fair is held in early October every year, and in Craftsbury Common, the annual Banjo Contest is held in late September. Sometimes they don't even wait for fall. Craftsbury Common hosts the New England Old Timers Fiddlers Contest, toward the end of July, that should not be missed for pure Vermont flavor.

Vermont has a wonderful variety of places to stay, from the quaint inns of Grafton to the very elegant Woodstock Inn in Woodstock. The Old Tavern in Grafton, for example, is a Vermont classic. It was built in 1801 and became a favorite New England resting place when purchased by the Phelps brothers in 1865. Rockers on the broad porch greet guests that have included Ulysses S. Grant, Henry David Thoreau, Nathaniel Hawthorne, Emerson and Oliver Wendell Holmes. Rudyard Kipling honeymooned there in 1892, with his bride Caroline Balestier. But, the Old Tavern is not exactly as it was back then. It's a restoration done by the Windham Foundation – and a meticulous job they've done, including the furniture, paintings and building itself. The bedrooms have canopied beds and fireplaces. Antique mirrors reflect fringed draperies, flowered wallpaper and crewel work bedspreads. The dining room once again serves hearty and plentiful food. Even the Grafton Cornet Band plays again on the village green.

Whether its Maine, Connecticut, Massachusetts, New Hampshire, Rhode Island or Vermont, they all have a unique flavor that is strictly New England and it includes liberty, independence and honor all mixed in with loyalty, pride and hard work.

But the heart of New England is also symbolized by a love of nature. Perhaps Longfellow's poems say it best. And perhaps through his "Song of Hiawatha" it's possible to better understand the ideals that shaped New England. Indian and white man both wanted to improve their lot and that of their fellow man. But the Indian, on one hand, was content to live within nature's protective cloak. The New Englander felt that nature was a test put there for him to tame, control and use.

"Round about the Indian village
Spread the meadows and the cornfields,
And beyond them stood the forest,
Stood the groves of singing pinetrees,
Green in Summer, white in Winter, . . .

In the Vale of Tawasentha,
In the green and silent valley.
'There he sang of Hiawatha,
Sang the Song of Hiawatha,
Sang his wondrous birth and being,
How he prayed and how he fasted,
How he lived, and toiled, and suffered,
That the tribes of men might prosper,
That he might advance his people!'

Ye who love the haunts of Nature,
Love the sunshine of the meadow,
Love the shadow of the forest,
Love the wind among the branches,
And the rain-shower and the snowstorm,
And the rushing of great rivers
Through their palisades of pinetrees,
And the thunder of the mountains,
Whose innumerable echoes
Flap like eagles in their eyries; –
Listen to these wild traditions,
To this Song of Hiawatha!

As shadows lengthen with the passing of the summer, the cool green colors of the New England countryside gradually submit to the inevitable rusty tones of fall *these pages.*

Barns, silos and the softly rounded hills of the north Vermont countryside appear to cower under the threat of a heavy, rain-charged sky *facing page*. Like an unwelcome intruder, the abandoned car *above* upsets the peace of the decaying farmyard.

As if touched by the brush of an inspired artist, the endless tones of copper, brown and gold suffuse the autumn woodland scene *left* with a warm glow that warns of winter's approach. It is at this time of the year that New England is at its most spectacular, attracting many thousands of wide-eyed tourists to the north-east. Sugar and syrup is extracted from the sap of the Vermont maple in the traditional manner in wooden sugarhouses *facing page* which can be seen dotting the agricultural parts of the state.

The weather-worn inscriptions on the tombstones that litter the slopes of the cemetery at Jericho *facing page* make interesting reading. *This page:* brightly painted clapboarded buildings in the colonial style are a feature of the southern Vermont town of Manchester.

As trees reluctantly shed their rustling foliage, a patchy coating of early snow covers the woodland scene *these pages*, warning of more severe weather ahead.

Brandon is one of the many unspoilt Vermont towns where life seems to continue at its own unhurried pace. The elegant and lovingly preserved houses, warm and welcoming under their quilts of snow *these pages*, reinforce the tranquil atmosphere.

Above: the dark shape of Mount Ethan Allen stands out against the darkening winter sky as purple clouds lend color to the land. *Facing page:* on cold, wind-free winter days the contours of Vermont's Green Mountains hide behind a veil of hanging mist.

The snow-packed rounded hills near Stowe in Vermont *facing page* become a hive of sporting activity in winter, with brightly dressed skiers flocking to the slopes in search of recreation.
A store of logs stacked ready for the grate *bottom left*, a terracotta-colored church against a cloudless sky *bottom center*, the lace like shapes of frozen, white-edged branches *below* and fresh-cut tracks in newly fallen snow *left* – all are common sights in New England's richly varied winter scenery.

Under a sullen sky, with the trees and hills encrusted in a coat of white, the whole of nature may appear curiously bereft of color *above,* and yet as soon as the wind shakes the branches, the vibrant tones of the evergreens breathe life into the surrounding hills *facing page.*

The colors of nature are an ever present inspiration to both poets and painters, and it is difficult to imagine anyone not being moved by the sights of New England in the fall. *Top left:* a typical New England covered bridge.

Fine-building preservation, careful development and an understanding of nature have led to the harmony that exists between Vermont towns and countryside, as at Woodstock *facing page* and Shelburne *below*.

Horses *facing page* are an important part of the nation's heritage and the Morgan Horse Farm *top right*, which belongs to the University of Vermont, has become famous as the home of the compact Morgan Horse – once the country's most popular all-purpose breed.
Right: a sea of freshly cut logs are left to season in the open air. With a large part of Vermont being forest land, it is not surprising that wood and wood products are an important part of the state's economy. Small farms *below*, while still common, are gradually being absorbed by the larger combines. *Bottom right:* a small rural community's roadside postboxes.

The New Hampshire vacation
resort of Indian Head offers the
visitor superb natural scenery
above and comfortable
accommodation in the fully-
equipped cabins *facing page*.

Granite from the massive 20 acre Rock of Ages quarries *left and far left* at Barre in Vermont, is processed at the modern Craftsman Center *above. Top right:* boats moored at Burlington, Vermont's largest city, on the shores of Lake Champlain. The 220 foot sidewheel steamer Ticonderoga *top center* is part of the transport exhibition at Shelburne's magnificent open-air museum, which also features the reconstructed general store building *top left*. *Facing page:* Coombs Beaver Brook Sugar House near Wilmington.

Franconia Notch, a deep valley some 6,500 acres in area, set between the Franconia and Kinsman Mountain ranges, is considered to be one of New Hampshires foremost attractions, with such magnificent features as the Flume *above right,* a spectacular 800 foot gorge, The Middle Kinsman Falls *above* and The Pool *facing page.*

Trimmed with a ribbon of nature's vivid colors, the rapid, rocky River Swift *left* flows through the autumn countryside of New England. Franconia Notch *facing page* echoes to the sound of water rushing along a boulder-strewn course, the granite bed polished smooth by thousands of years of incessant action.
Overleaf left: the charming, white, weather-boarded Episcopal Church of St. Mathew at Sugar Hill. *Remaining pictures:* the dense woodland, scenic falls and rock formations of Pinkham Notch in the White Mountains of New Hampshire.

The languid, lapping waters of Lake Winnipesaukee *right and facing page* cover an area of 72 square miles and are surrounded by some of New Hampshire's most beautiful countryside. The lake itself is a popular summer recreation area with a steamboat service and annual regatta.

With the White Mountains for a backbone, the Granite State is a land of heavily wooded slopes *below*, rugged valleys and a profusion of rivers, lakes and ponds. One of the 13 original states of the Union, New Hampshire is a region very much tied to the past while looking to the future. Towns such as Tufton Corner *left* exercise a unique form of democracy through a system of town meetings where, rather than delegate, inhabitants can participate in decision making.

Constructed from the rock on which it stands, the magnificent granite Statehouse at Concord *top left,* New Hampshire's capital, boasts of being the country's oldest. Lovingly preserved by the New Hampshire Historical Society, the Concord coach *left* is a reminder of the recent past, while the Old Country Store in Moultonboro *far left and above* combines history with old-fashioned service. *Center left:* the shores of the Atlantic near Hampton Beach. *Facing page:* a typical covered or 'kissing' bridge at Blair, over the Beebe River.

New England's craggy coastline, scene of innumerable marine disasters, is studded with lighthouses whose flashing beacons guide the passing ships. Known as the 'Boating Capital of New England', Boothbay Harbor *facing page* is Maine's prime summer playground; its history steeped in ships and sailing.

Gently rolling fishing boats and pleasure craft lie at anchor along the sparkling wharves of **Boothbay Harbor** *these pages.* The resort offers the visitor an unparalleled selection of boating activities that range from river and ocean cruising to deep sea fishing. For those who prefer to stay on land, the quaint, winding village streets hold their own attractions.

Silhouetted against the setting sun, fishing craft rest on
the gently rippling surface of **Boothbay Harbor** *above.*
Facing page: **picturesque Newagen seen from the
Boothbays.**

Measured from north to south Maine's coastline amounts to only some 250 miles, however, by clinging to the deeply indented shores the distance comes to over 3000 miles. Among the stunningly beautiful inlets are the picturesque bay *facing page* and the wooded shores of Northeast Harbor *above*.

The rich forests of Maine, which still cover over three-quarters of the land area have, since the time of the earliest settlers, been an important source of income. The timber was used in the construction of houses and towns and, despite the ravages of time and fire, many of the earlier structures still survive. Before the advent of steel-hulled vessels, ship and boat-building was a flourishing industry. The glass-like surface of the Androscoggin River at Rumford mirrors the shapes of the house and surrounding vegetation *facing page.*

Carved by the action of prehistoric glaciers and the incessant pounding of the seas, the rocky outcrops along Maine's scenic coast form firm foundations for the many lighthouses *these pages.*

The cliffs of Cape Elizabeth rise from the foaming waters of the Atlantic Ocean *right.* It is easy to forget the fury that the Bass Harbor Lighthouse often has to face, when it is seen in the peaceful light of a summer evening *above and facing page. Top right:* **the Portland Head Lighthouse can trace its origins back to 1791.**

Capital of Maine, the largest of the six New England states, is Augusta, a relatively small city of some 22,000 people, perched on the banks of the Kennebec River. The town's first permanent building, Fort Western, was built in 1754 for protection against Indian attacks. Restored in 1921, the fort now serves as a museum *left and bottom left. Far left, below and facing page:* shades of white and green dominate Wiscasset, a charming town nestling on the hillside by the River Sheepscot. Although located some 12 miles from the sea, Wiscasset boasts one of Maine's deepest harbors, and it was once an important seafaring town.

Distinguished-looking red brick public buildings, such as those in Bath's Washington Street *facing page,* are as much a part of Maine's architectural heritage as the typical timber faced houses, shops and churches *this page.*

Littered with autumn debris, the waters of one of Maine's many lakes *above* echo the colors of the trees and sky. *Facing page:* the Hamilton Laboratory Farm Buildings in Acadia National Park.

St. John's Catholic Church at Bangor *top* is noted for its pipe organ as well as the beautiful Tyrolean stained-glass window *far right*. The improbably named Kennebunkport *top right* is a small but popular summer resort. *Right and facing page:* lobster floats, traps and a sea of assorted junk surround a crumbling building in Owl's Head. *Above:* the shifting dunes of the "Desert of Maine," near Freeport, cover an area that was prosperous farming land in the 19th century.

Made of white Georgia marble, the imposing State Capitol in Providence, Rhode Island *below right* boasts one of the world's largest unsupported marble domes, second only in size to that of St. Peter's in Rome. As well as being a busy commercial center, Providence is also an important deep water port *top right*. Situated at the southern tip of Rhode Island is Newport, a city with a fine naval tradition *below*. Newport Bridge *facing page* arches gracefully over a shimmering sea.

New Haven, Connecticut, is the home of Yale University, one of the nation's oldest and most respected seats of learning *this page and facing page bottom left and center.* The remaining pictures show colorful scenes of New Haven pageantry.

The soaring spires, ivy-clad walls and stone-mullioned and leaded windows of Yale University's venerable old buildings convey a sense of permanence and studious peace. Founded in 1701 and moved to its present site five years later, the university was named after Elihu Yale, the benefactor who, in 1718, made a substantial donation to what was then a college. In 1887 the institution was invested with University status, but it was not until 1969 that women were finally admitted as students.
As well as being able to visit the university's fine museums, gallery and libraries, the visitor to Yale can take advantage of the free guided tours around the campus.

Streaked by the reflections of the lights from office buildings that line her banks, the Connecticut River *above* flows through the city of Hartford, the state capital. Many of Hartford's older, run-down buildings were demolished during a massive redevelopment program, but fine old structures such as the majestic, gold-domed Capitol, *facing page* which sits in Bushnell Park, continue to grace the skyline.

Reflecting the glories of New England's past, the beautiful village of Mystic Seaport *these pages* **is an authentic recreation of a 19th century coastal town, with tall-masted sailing ships and a whaler anchored in the harbor. Period shops and buildings were brought here from other parts of the state by the Marine Historical Association which created this living museum.**

The rolling hills and rocky, tree-lined river valleys *left* that form much of the Connecticut countryside, are dotted with the occasional quaint old town or village. Early settlers who came to the state hoping to gain a living from the land soon discovered that, except for the relatively fertile areas surrounding the Connecticut River, the soil was uncooperative and, not surprisingly, farmsteads such as those pictured *below and facing page* are an infrequent sight. Not to be deterred, the enterprising inhabitants of Connecticut turned their skills, echoed in the splendid covered bridge *below left,* to industry and the state flourished as a center of manufacture and commerce.

Appealing sights such as the Congregational Church at Litchfield Green *top left*, Nook Farm, Mark Twain's Victorian mansion *above*, the old stone house in Guildford *top right* and the weather-boarded houses such as the one in Cheshire *top center*, blend with the splendors of the countryside *facing page* to give Connecticut its distinctive character. *Left:* the Connestoga wagon, a reminder of the pioneering spirit of the state's first settlers.

The city of Boston *above*, seen across an ice-packed Charles River, glows golden in the rays of a setting winter sun. *Facing page:* the gilded dome of the State House overlooks Boston's old residential area from its lofty perch on Beacon Hill.

Located across the Charles River from Boston is the town of Cambridge, best known as the home of Harvard *this page*, America's oldest University. Founded in 1636, the college takes its name from the Puritan benefactor who bequeathed half of his library and estate to the institution. John Harvard's statue *top center* commemorates this act of generosity. Harvard Yard *left* stands at the center of what was the original college. The Memorial Church *facing page* was constructed as a war memorial in 1932.

The light-flecked shapes of Boston's skyscrapers create impressionistic reflections on the surface of the Charles River *above*. The massive 52-story Prudential Center shown left of picture, as well as being visible from miles around, offers superb views of Massachusetts and beyond, from the observation deck on the 50th floor. Moored at Griffith's Wharf *facing page*, a replica of the Brig Beaver II recalls the historic Boston Tea Party incident.

Quincy Market *these pages* was built in 1826 under the direction of the then mayor of Boston Josiah Quincy. Intended as a replacement for Faneuil Hall *top left and center* which stands in Dock Square, the market has undergone considerable changes in the ensuing years although its essential character has been preserved. It is now one of the city's many attractive focal points.

The blazing trails of homeward-bound cars weave
iridescent patterns over the streets and bridges of a night-
bound city *these pages*. At dusk the Boston skyline is a sea
of glittering lights.

Aerial views of Boston and its surroundings *these pages* with the Charles River and the Bay beyond dominating the scene. The picture *facing page* includes a crowded Fenway Park, home of the famous Red Sox baseball team.

Facing page: **Boston's Public Garden** *top left and bottom left* **stands at the heart of the Downtown area, and is famous for the Swanboats on its lake as well as the fine monuments, such as the equestrian statue of George Washington** *bottom right. Top right* **is the Neo-Romanesque style Trinity Church on Copley Square.** *This page:* **Beacon Hill** *top right and bottom,* **located on the northern side of Boston Common, is the oldest residential area in the city, its narrow, gas-lit, cobbled streets lined with proud old brownstone houses.** *Top left:* **Copp's Hill Burial Ground, the city's second oldest cemetery.** *Top center:* **the Old West Church.**

Classical, Romanesque, colonial and ultra-modern; the varied styles of Boston architecture *these pages* somehow blend together to achieve a rare and pleasing harmony.

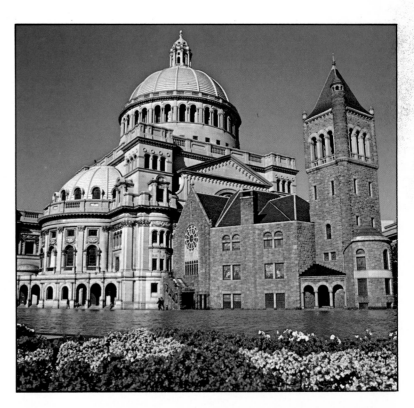

Criss-crossed with paths and footways, Boston Common *above,* bordered by Beacon Street to the left and Tremont to the right, is the green lung of this pleasant city. The tower and the satelite shops, offices and apartment buildings that comprise the Prudential Center, dominate the aerial view *facing page.* At the lower right of the picture can be seen the domed Renaissance-style church of the Christian Science Center.

The sparkling, wind-swept waters of the Harbor and Charles River *facing page, below and far right* **play host to countless pleasure craft.** *Bottom:* **Boston's Downtown skyline from the deck of a ship.** *Right and bottom right:* **The USS Constitution stands in the Naval Shipyard at Charlestown.**

Settled in around 1669, Deerfield, Massachusetts *above*, a small village of some 30 buildings, is famous for its restored Heritage Foundation Houses which are open to the public. Framed by the russet colors of fall, the white boarded house *facing page* stands in Duxbury, a Massachusetts coastal town that boasts one of New England's finest beaches.

Razed to the ground by repeated Indian attacks between 1672-1704, the village of
Deerfield underwent a series of re-births. The existing buildings, such as the Sheldon-
Hawks House *above* and the Ashley House *facing page* which dates from 1732, are
carefully maintained as part of the National Historic District village.

Small bays, inlets, beaches and the undulating countryside of Massachusetts; all are transformed by winter's blanket of snow, made sparkling by sunshine and blue skies at Duxbury *above, top left and facing page,* **and Deerfield** *left and top right.*

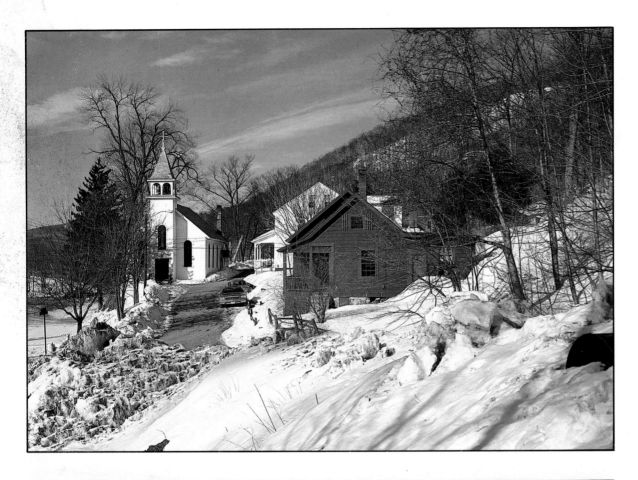

Whilst there can be no denying that New England towns and countryside are at their most picturesque in the fall, the crisp, clear air and vivid blue skies of a fine winter's day lend an appealing greeting-card quality to scenes such as these.

On December 21st 1620, the Pilgrims landed at Plymouth to become the first permanent settlers in America north of Virginia. The original rock at which they landed is enshrined in the Plymouth Rock Memorial *bottom left* to protect it from souvenir hunters. In the harbor nearby, is moored an exact replica of the Mayflower which commemorates the historic voyage *facing page. Left and below:* The Dwight-Barnard House Museum at Deerfield.

Endless miles of grassy, rolling sand-dunes *above* edge the shores of Cape Cod, making the area particularly popular with summer tourists. *Facing page:* a tranquil Buzzard's Bay at sunset.

Provincetown *these pages*, **on the tip of Cape Cod's curved finger, is the point at which the Pilgrims first set foot in the New World before crossing the Bay to Plymouth. Once an important whaling port, the town still relies on fishing for its livelihood.**

Sand cliffs, topped by grass and scrubland, rise from the deserted Nauset Beach, with Nauset Beach Lighthouse in the distance *above. Facing page:* **Sandwich**, with Mill Creek Marsh in the foreground, has the distinction of being the Cape's oldest and one of her most attractive towns. It is particularly famous for the colored glass that was made here in the 19th century.

The largest of New England's islands, the imaginatively-named Martha's Vineyard *these pages,* is a 7-mile ferry ride from Woods Hole on the Massachusetts mainland. Settled in the early 17th century, the island flourished as a whaling port – today, the major industries are fishing and tourism. *Right, top right and facing page:* the harbor of Menemsha. The "On-Time" ferry *above* links Edgartown with the sandy island of Chappaquiddick where the Dyke Bridge *top left* is located.

The coastline scenery of the Vineyard is remarkably varied, with gently rising beaches giving way to majestic, grass-topped cliffs *above* and strangely-colored clay formations *top left and facing page. Far left:* logged tree-trunks weather on the beach. *Top right:* Menemsha Harbor and the Edgartown Lighthouse *left.*

The lighthouses of Cape Cod and its neighboring islands overlook the unpredictable waters that surround their shores. The Chatham *far right* and Provincetown *below* beacons, stand on the mainland while those at Brandt Point *bottom right* and Sankaty Head *bottom far right* guide shipping around Nantucket island. *Facing page:* the coastguard station at Coastguard Beach and *right* the town hall at Brewster on Cape Cod.

The simple, natural beauty with which Cape Cod and her islands have been blessed *these pages,* makes the region ever popular with New Englanders eager to escape the pressures of city life.

Named in memory of the Italian scientist who in 1901 made the first trans-Atlantic radio transmission, Marconi Beach *facing page,* with its weather-sculpted low sandy cliffs, stretches past Wellfleet on Cape Cod. *Far left:* the jagged Nashaquista Cliffs at Gay Head, Martha's Vineyard. The desert-like shifting sands of Provincelands *below* and at Race Point Beach *bottom left* form part of the Cape's Atlantic coastline and as part of the National Seashore Project they are a protected natural resource. *Left:* dunes on Dionis Beach, Nantucket Island.

A hazy sun shines on the rows of beach huts that line the shore at Provincetown *left*, while the picture *below right* shows the wooden walkway that forms part of the Fort Hill swamp trail at Eastham. The summit of the Pilgrim Monument gives superb views of Provincetown and the Bay *facing page. Bottom left:* the kitchen of the Jethro Coffin house on Nantucket. *Bottom right:* the horse-breeding farm at West Tisbury, and *below center* the Federated Church at Edgartown. *Overleaf:* the seemingly endless beaches are just one of the Cape's many varied attractions.

INDEX